Whiting Williams was a prosperous, educated, turn-of-the-century Ohio businessman who adopted the guise of a blue-collar worker in order to learn firsthand about labor conditions. He used this information to improve labor conditions and salary during an era marked by the birth of modern industrialization, labor-management dichotomy, labor unions, strikes of historic proportions, strikebreakers, massive unemployment, and formal labor-management relations.

The book focuses on Williams in the 1920s and 1930s as he traveled America, Great Britain, France, Germany, and Russia. As he worked alongside laborers, he developed theories about work and attitudes toward it. These experiences also provided the material for comparative studies of workers in various nations, regions, and local societies. He addressed industrialists in lectures and writings directed toward improving workers' lives.

This biography traces the life of a pioneer in the study of labor and management whose insights ultimately helped lay the foundation for modern work environments and workers' rights.

White Collar Hobo

White Collar Hobo

THE TRAVELS OF WHITING WILLIAMS

Daniel A. Wren

Iowa State University Press / Ames

DANIEL A. WREN is Professor of Management and Curator, Harry W. Bass Business History Collection, The University of Oklahoma.

© 1987 Iowa State University Press, Ames, Iowa 50010. All rights reserved. Composed by Iowa State University Press from author-provided disks. Printed in the United States of America

Title page photos from *Full Up and Fed Up: The Worker's Mind in Crowded Britain,* Charles Scribner's Sons, 1921

First edition, 1987

Library of Congress Cataloging-in-Publication Data

Wren, Daniel A.
   White collar hobo.

   Bibliography: p.
   Includes index.
   1. Williams, Whiting, 1878–   . 2. Labor and laboring classes – United States – Biography. 3. Personnel directors – United States – Biography. 4. Industrial relations – United States. I. Title.
HD8073.W47W74   1987   331'.092'4 [B]   87–4048
ISBN 0–8138–1922–9

Contents

Preface

WHEN I first interviewed Dorothy Rogers Williams and told her of my plans to prepare a biography of her late husband, she clasped her hands gleefully and said "Whiting would have liked that!" Since that interview, I have learned of the death of Mrs. Williams, but the enthusiasm she showed for this project sustained me in many ways. It is difficult to capture on paper an image to match Whiting Williams in life. Williams lived almost a century, wrote prolifically, and traveled incessantly. He came to his professional maturity relatively late in life, but he more than compensated for this with his longevity and productivity. He was a venturesome man — one who left the relative comfort of a white collar executive's office to put on worker's clothes and find out what was on the worker's mind. He was also a perceptive observer — his insights into the importance of work to a person, the social scheme of industrial life, the appeal of unions, and other ideas mark him as one who could capture the relevant issues and express them so others could learn. Finally, he was a sensitive man — one who elevated the importance of the individual, extended that into the significance of our relations with others, and offered all of us a lesson in how to handle our interpersonal dealings. While these do not exhaust his finer qualities, they provide standards for our own aspirations.

The making of this story has benefited from the efforts of many people. Foremost among them is Dorothy Rogers Williams, who graciously took me on a grand tour of their home and told of the life of her husband. Harter Whiting Williams also shared his ideas and was willing to reflect on what I had written of his father and the family.

This research would not have been possible if Williams had not left his personal and business papers to the Western Reserve Historical Society in Cleveland, Ohio. The staff there has done a marvelous job of sorting, classifying, and preserving the large amount of material. To James B. Casey, Charles Sherrill, and the reference staff, many thanks.

For the early inspiration to do this project, credit must be given to the late Richard J. Whiting of California State University at Los

Angeles. Dick's interest in human relations "links" and his research on Paul Goehre provided a touchstone for this work on Whiting Williams. Numerous individuals who knew and worked with Williams were also very helpful: Allan H. Mogensen, founder and director of the Work Simplification Conferences, provided a series of tapes of Williams's presentations; Fred Kersting provided unpublished material; A. B. Cummins, professor emeritus, Case Western Reserve University, also sent materials; James C. Worthy, Northwestern University, provided recollections of Williams and his appearances as a teacher-lecturer; Emil Walter-Busch, University of St. Gallen, Switzerland, provided information on Williams and Dean Wallace B. Donham at Harvard University; and Meredith B. Colket, Jr., curator emeritus of the Western Reserve Historical Society, took the time to reflect on his long association with Williams. Pat Mills, of the University of Oklahoma Library, patiently kept materials flowing through interlibrary loan; Charles Broadway did some early bibliographical digging; and Muriel Hatcher typed the first draft of the manuscript. Others who provided useful information about Williams include Mary Jo Jones, librarian for Western Electric; Burleigh Gardner and Fred Wickert, early employees of Western Electric; Charles Wrege of Rutgers University; Ron Greenwood of the General Motors Institute; Bill Fox of the University of Florida; and Morrell Heald of Case Western Reserve University. To University of Oklahoma administrators Larry McKibbin and Sul Lee, I also offer my hearty thanks. Special thanks should go to Mary McClain and the entire IPC staff for the careful word processing of the final copy.

Introduction

THE latter one-third of the nineteenth century in America was characterized by national economic expansion, by rapid technological advancement, and by the growth of large-scale enterprise. The American economy had developed slowly after gaining its independence from Great Britain. The late eighteenth and early nineteenth centuries were characterized by developments in textiles, canals, wooden turnpikes, the telegraph, and the railroads. Most organizations were small, technologically underdeveloped, and family owned and managed. These were managed with little or no hierarchy of authority. Management was personal; the small number of employees and the personal leadership of the owner made the organization close-knit. Grievances could be heard, problems worked out, and benefits provided on a person-to-person basis. The family firm was adequate to the task it faced at the time.

As the railroads pushed their way west, the nation was finally bound coast-to-coast by a web of steel rails and a communication system of telegraph lines. The cable under the Atlantic Ocean brought Europe and America just minutes rather than months apart. These developments in transportation and communication opened new markets and, coupled with emerging processes for industrial production, enabled a spurt in the growth of American business. As organizations grew to capitalize upon the developing technologies and the emerging markets, their size exceeded the grasp of the family firm of the past. Large-scale enterprise needed skilled managers to develop plans, to design organizations, to select the right employees, to lead and motivate them, and to measure and control their performance.

This transition from the family firm of the past to the large enterprise of today was one of trial-and-error, as managers attempted to solve what was referred to as the "labor question." Labor violence in the 1880s and 1890s fueled public fears of unions. The Molly Maguires terrorized the populace with murders and other atrocities in the Pennsylvania coal fields. The Haymarket Affair (1886), in which the Knights of Labor tried to enforce a general strike in Chicago, led to several deaths. The Homestead strike (1892) and the Pullman strike (1894) were other examples of violence brought about by confrontations between labor and management. Public fear of "radicals" and "anarchists," who were often equated with legitimate union organizers, kept the union movement at a relative standstill. One success was the American Federation of Labor, organized in 1886 as a federation of craft unions that concentrated on the pursuit of immediate economic gains for the worker on the job rather than on distant political reforms. Under Samuel Gompers's leadership, the union's membership increased from fewer than 200,000 in 1886 to more than 2,865,000 at the time of Gompers's death in 1924.

The industrial response to labor-management problems was built upon such familial traditions of the past as "industrial betterment" or "welfare work." The first recorded attempt to establish an office for welfare work appears to have been at the National Cash Register Company in 1897. The company's founder and president, John H. Patterson, appointed Lena H. Tracy as the firm's first "welfare director." Joseph Bancroft and Sons had a "welfare secretary" in 1899 and the H. J. Heinz Company employed a "social secretary" in 1902, as did the Colorado Fuel and Iron Company in 1901 and the International Harvester Company in 1903. Others would include Filene Department Stores, the Natural Food Company, Plymouth Cordage, John B. Stetson Company, Westinghouse Electric, and more.

The job of the welfare secretary was to improve the lives of workers both off and on the job, hence the terms "welfare" and "industrial betterment." The welfare secretary listened to and handled grievances, ran the workshop "sick room," provided for recreation and education, arranged transfers for dissatisfied workers, administered the dining facilities, prepared nutritious menus, and looked after the moral behavior of unmarried female factory employees.

Another early twentieth-century approach to the problems of labor-management relations was put forth by the "scientific management" movement and its polestar, Frederick W. Taylor. Taylor described the duties of the "shop disciplinarian" as selecting and discharging employees, keeping performance records, handling disciplinary problems, administering wage payments, and serving as a "peacemaker." Although Taylor described many of the tasks of an employment department, he did little to advance personnel practice, leaving that to his followers. In recognizing the need for an employment specialist, however, Taylor did prepare the way for the emergence of personnel as a staff rather than line task, as had been the previous practice.

About 1910 the phrase "welfare work" began to waver as the scientific management movement became more widely known. Scientific management also gave impetus to the industrial psychology of Hugo Munsterberg, leading to an increased interest in employee testing, vocational guidance, and employee placement.

The path to melding welfare work, industrial psychology, and scientific management was not a smooth one. The personnel departments of many firms were more often than not an uneven mixture of welfarism, psychological testing, and scientific management techniques such as job analysis.

The growing concern for standardizing and improving personnel practices led to the first professional associations for personnel staff specialists. The first national organization to deal with personnel matters was the National Association of Corporation Schools, founded in 1913 to advance the training and education of industrial employees. The second national organization, the National Association of Employment Managers, grew out of a local Employment Managers Association started in Boston by Meyer Bloomfield. In 1922, these two groups (NACS and NAEM) merged to form the National Personnel Association.

Harlow S. Person introduced the first opportunity for college training of employment managers at Dartmouth's Tuck School of Administration and Finance as early as 1915. Those who wished to become employment managers took Tuck's graduate business program but had the opportunity to prepare a thesis which solved a specific problem of management in a specific plant.

Despite rising professionalism, personnel practices of the early 1900s continued to reflect a mixture of welfarism and efficiency in this time of transition. For example, Henry Ford, faced with a tight labor market and a worker turnover rate of 10 percent, formed an early employment department in 1914 called the "Sociological Department." This sociological experiment lasted but three years and ended when Mr. Ford told Samuel S. Marquis, head of the department, that there was too much snooping around in people's private lives. Thereafter, the Ford Motor Company turned its attention to advising and educating the employees. It has been estimated that as many employment departments were created during 1919-1920 as had been created in all years previously. Employers could see the success of Henry Ford and conclude that this added concern for their personnel led to a greater prosperity for all, labor and management.

It was this milieu of concern for understanding the worker and for improving personnel practices that set the stage for Whiting Williams. Williams was born into a relatively prosperous family, received his A.B. and M.A. degrees from Oberlin College, and tried his hand at various jobs before becoming vice-president and director of personnel for the Hydraulic Pressed Steel Company of Cleveland, Ohio. At Oberlin, Williams was exposed thoroughly to the Social Gospel, a liberal, socially conscious Protestantism that asked people to accept as their life calling the improvement of social conditions, including those in industry. Williams decided to apply the Social Gospel idea of direct involvement, so he shed his white collar and headed out in the disguise of a worker to study industrial conditions firsthand. He felt the only way to discover the human problems of industry would be to become a participant-observer, because human behavior sprang from people's feelings and one had to feel as they felt to understand fully the condition of the worker.

From this shirt sleeve empiricism, Williams would make a career of lecturing, consulting, and writing of his experiences as a worker. From time to time, he would resume his worker's disguise to study strikers and strikebreakers, unemployment, and labor-management relations in Great Britain, Europe, and much of the industrialized world. From this would come a number of insights that mark Williams as a pioneer in the study of work, working, the worker, and management. The travels of this white collar hobo are the story of people at work as told by one who was working beside them.

White Collar Hobo

ONE

The Making of a Hobo

IN JANUARY 1919, a man dressed in worker's clothing and calling himself "Charlie Heitman" boarded a train in Cleveland, bound for Pittsburgh. Claiming to be unemployed and to have only twenty-five dollars in his pocket, "Charlie" was far from what he appeared to be. His real name was Whiting Williams; he had been born into a prosperous family, was well educated, and his most recent working clothes had been those of a white collar executive. Why the disguise? What had led Whiting Williams to these pretenses?

Family Background

This train passenger of 1919 was born Charles Whiting Williams on March 11, 1878, in Shelby, Ohio. His father, Benjamin J. Williams, was born in Marion, Ohio, June 23, 1842. As a young man, Benjamin had sought his fortune in the "far west," St. Louis, Missouri. When the Civil War began, Benjamin served in Major Ink's St. Louis battalion on the Union side. When his one year's enlistment expired, he returned to Ohio where he enlisted in the Ninety-sixth Regiment of Ohio Volunteers. Attached to the Army of the Tennessee, the ninety-sixth regiment served under General Ulysses S. Grant during the siege of Vicksburg. After the war, Benjamin J. Williams returned to Ohio, married Ida Whiting on December 24, 1868, and settled with her in Shelby, Ohio. Benjamin was an enterprising individual who was a cofounder of the First National Bank of Shelby, the Shelby Waterworks, the Shelby Seamless Steel Company, and the Easy Spring Hinge Company.

Ida Whiting was born in 1849 in Buffalo, New York, the daughter of D. W. and Susan (Page) Whiting. The Whiting family had origi-

3

nally settled in Connecticut in the seventeenth century and had a tradition of involvement in patriotic service since the period of the American Revolutionary War. Ida Whiting was a talented painter of china and an accomplished musician. Her marriage to Benjamin J. Williams resulted in the birth of four children: Florence, Lucia, Beatty, and Charles Whiting Williams.[1]

In later years, Whiting Williams would recall that he "was lucky to be born in a small town—nobody was anonymous, everybody was responsible."[2] In this midwestern American town of the nineteenth century, Williams would absorb a lifelong credo of individual responsibility within a community setting. Shelby, Ohio, was a "town small enough to make church and school into powerful expecters [of both good moral behavior and achievement]."[3] Because his father was a successful businessman in the community, Whiting Williams felt that even more was expected of him in terms of behavior and performance in school. From these expectations would evolve another lifelong value: that one's lifework provide a definition of who and what one was for both oneself and for others. Above all, work was essential to a person's well-being.

Williams's sense of enterprise emerged early when he signed on as the Shelby agent for the Troy Laundry Company of Troy, Ohio. He gathered his clients' dirty laundry on Mondays, took it to the train station for pickup by the New York Central Railroad, and returned the clean laundry to his clients on Fridays. His sense of thrift was also encouraged as he deposited his weekly profits in a savings account in his father's bank.

The young Williams was seen by his peers and by his teachers and church leaders as responsible, earnest, and well-behaved. He was active in the youth programs of the Epworth League of the Methodist Church and sang in the choir. He recalled that the church encouraged "testifying" as a worthy calling, and there was an unspoken assumption in the family and among others that he would become a minister. For Charles Whiting Williams, Shelby High School class of 1894, it was decided that the best place to prepare for his calling was at Oberlin College.

Oberlin College and the Social Gospel

Oberlin College was founded in 1833 in Ohio's Western Reserve region to train young people to spread the message of salvation on

America's western frontier. Named after Jean Frédéric Oberlin, who renounced worldly pleasures to help the poor in Alsace (on the eastern border of present-day France), Oberlin College was to be a model of Christian piety for the people of the great Northwest Territory. In spirit and deed, Oberlin was considered to be on the leading edge of the social questions of the day. It was the first coeducational college in the United States, as well as the first to admit blacks.

Oberlin College was in a stage of religious and intellectual ferment when Charles Whiting Williams arrived there in the fall of 1894. Darwinism and its corollary, Social Darwinism, had become quite popular on the Oberlin campus after Charles Darwin's publication of *The Origin of the Species* in 1859. Students and faculty debated widely the implications of evolution for science, as well as for faith. The basic conclusion was that evolution and Christianity were compatible, one dealing with the body and one with the spirit. As long as science and religion were separate, there would be no problems. A perpetual tendency for improvement in the human condition was inherent in evolution, so the task of faith was to work to bring about a concomitant improvement in spirtual conditions.[4]

While Darwinism led to a surge of science in classrooms and laboratories at Oberlin, the more widespread impact was involvement in the emerging "Social Gospel" movement. The Social Gospel was a liberal, socially conscious Protestantism that originated early in the Gilded Age as a precursor to progressivism.[5] The Social Gospel was Christianity in action in society; hence, the phrase *social Christianity* was a call for all Christians to go beyond concern for salvation and become involved in reforming society's problems. Bad social conditions were the result of human ignorance and indifference rather than of natural laws. Rather than awaiting the gradual improvement promised by the social Darwinists, the social Christian had a moral duty to change things through philanthropy, lobbying for legislation, education, and reform movements such as Prohibition, community social welfare, and other forces of change.

Walter Rauschenbusch and Washington Gladden were two of the pioneers in formulating the Social Gospel. Gladden, a Columbus, Ohio, minister, articulated the major social problems of the times as labor unrest, intemperance, poverty, slums, and child and female labor.[6] Solutions for labor unrest resided largely in organizing the workers into strong unions to resist employers, gaining profit-sharing plans for workers, and requiring arbitration of labor-management disputes. Temperance was essential: the greatest evil for workers was alcohol because of its contribution to poverty and a subsequent ever-widening circle of effects such as slums, family disintegration, and other social evils. Some social problems—for example, child and female labor—could be dealt with only through legislation.

Oberlin alumni and faculty were also involved in social Christianity. Howard Hyde Russell, an Oberlin alumnus, founded the Oberlin Temperance Alliance and the Ohio Anti-Saloon League. John Rogers Commons, class of 1888 and a faculty member from 1891 to 1892, became famous for his accomplishments as a labor historian, economist, and social reformer at the University of Wisconsin. As editor of the Oberlin student newspaper, Commons had advocated involvement in social problems and had recommended "putting ourselves in the place of the working man" in order to know his problems by "personal contact."[7]

Both Russell and Commons would leave their mark on Williams, who remained active in the Oberlin alumni group throughout his lifetime. An ardent Prohibitionist, Williams would find a spark in the concern of the social Christians concerning "drink" as the working man's curse. From Commons, Williams would put into practice the idea of gaining understanding by becoming involved as a participant. While Russell and Commons inspired the young Williams, two other activists in the Social Gospel movement, Henry Churchill King and Graham Taylor, touched his life more directly.[8] King had been a widely respected teacher at Oberlin before he became president of the college in 1903. As a faculty member, King was the acknowledged leader of the "liberals," the Oberlin proponents of the Social Gospel who taught that service to society and the solution of social problems should be the aims of all Christians. As president of Oberlin from 1903 to 1927, King continued the "progressive" goals of education for social service. His assistant for eight of the years of his tenure was Charles Whiting Williams.

Graham Taylor, another leading Social Gospel clergyman, headed the Department of Christian Sociology at the Chicago Theological Seminary (which became the Divinity School of the University of Chicago in 1895).[9] Taylor's influence on Williams began with Taylor's involvement in Oberlin's Institute of Christian Sociology. Beginning in 1894, the institute sponsored leading Social Gospel speakers for on-campus appearances. For example, in 1895 the theme was "The Causes and Proposed Remedies for Poverty," and the speakers included such notables as the economist John Bates Clark of Amherst, the lawyer Clarence Darrow, Jane Addams of Chicago's Hull House, and Samuel Gompers, president of the American Federation of Labor. Other speakers during Williams's stay at Oberlin included Washington Gladden, Lincoln Steffens, Charles A. Beard, Robert M. La-Follette, Jack London, and Walter Rauschenbusch.[10] Graham Taylor would later attract Williams to the University of Chicago to study theology.

The Social Gospel at Oberlin asked that individuals transcend their search for personal salvation to reach for the reform of existing social, economic, and political conditions. Williams was taught to see the world as one large mission field, and he hoped to serve "to please God by serving at least a few others, or if not, then to serve no less than God himself."[11] At Oberlin, this seedbed of social Christianity, Charles Whiting Williams developed his drive to study and propose remedies for social and economic problems.

Berlin and Chicago

Whiting Williams had a passion for travel. One of his earliest recorded trips was a visit to the Chicago World's Fair of 1893, financed exclusively with savings from his laundry pickup and delivery service. After his junior year at Oberlin, he and his brother, Beatty, voiced a desire to travel to Europe. Their father, Benjamin J. Williams, offered them each $100 for such a trip, provided they promised not to smoke cigarettes until they were at least twenty-one years of age.[12] Knowing that $100 apiece would not finance the entire trip, Whiting discovered that "so long as a chap had stout shoulders and knew one end of a manure fork from the other," one could work for a transatlantic passage on a cattle boat.[13] With their father's money and their manure forks in hand, Beatty and Whiting took a cattle boat to Liverpool, England, in the summer of 1898 and, to save money, walked the remaining 200 miles to London. From that time forward, Whiting Williams seemed to have a suitcase in one hand and a travel ticket in the other.

When Williams was graduated from Oberlin College in 1899, he still intended to enter the ministry. At age twenty-one, however, it was generally agreed that he needed some seasoning, perhaps an associate pastorate in a small church or graduate work in some theological seminary, or perhaps some travel. Williams's predilection for travel won the day: "With no decision apparent, I went abroad to think about my future."[14] He called this his *wanderjähre*, meaning "a time to travel and reflect." He chose Berlin and its famous university as his home base when his professor, Henry C. King, who had spent a sabbatical there from 1893 to 1894, recommended it for its culture and its large colony of almost 2500 other American student-travelers. Williams hoped that his exposure to "the study of human nature in Europe" would aid in future decisions concerning the development of his career.

His Berlin experience did enrich his study of human nature. He was appalled by the carefree attitude students had toward studying and going to classes. Professors' lectures were sparsely attended and no one, including the professors, seemed to take this matter seriously. Furthermore, the German scholars saw manual labor as a disgrace— the social class one belonged to was based largely on education and there was a big difference between those who were workers and the rest of society. Williams, who had spent a summer in the mill of the Shelby Seamless Steel Company, who had shoveled his way across the Atlantic, and who had handled dirty laundry, saw no shame in work but saw it, rather, as a point in one's favor, even for a banker's son. Even at this early time in his life, he began to note in his diary the different occupations he observed, the salaries they brought, and the opportunities they presented for people. Another cultural shock occurred when he observed that the Germans drank "too much champagne" and other alcoholic beverages. Perhaps his greatest reproof was his description of Berliners as *Gottlos*, or "ungodly." From their lack of attention to their studies to their scorn for work, their intemperance, and their ungodliness, Williams found the Berliners utterly devoid of any redeeming social virtues. One can sense the biblical phrase "Get thee behind me, Satan" when Williams entered in his diary that one "must fight this [ungodliness, etc.] if one is among the Germans in Berlin."[15]

While Berlin offered temptations, it also offered cultural opportunities that Williams found pleasing. He became an admirer of the work of the composer Richard Wagner and attended operas and concerts when and where possible. Art and sculpture also abounded, as well as museums. While the snow of winter still lingered in Berlin in the spring of 1900, he headed south with recorded stopovers in Dresden, Nuremberg, Innsbruck, Verona, Florence, Venice, and Rome. In Florence he wrote of his love for the paintings he saw by Rubens, Titian, Van Dyck, and, especially, Raphael. In Venice he described the architecture in the Piazza San Marco, noting how the square was "filled by the rising moon" and was "one of the most brilliant sights I

have ever looked upon." In Rome he observed the rich art treasures
and remarked, "You don't know Christian art until you have seen the
Sistine Chapel."[16]

Whereas Berlin had been disappointing in a religious sense, this
trip through Italy restored Williams's sense of mission. His *wanderjähre* over, Williams was ready for what he called his "seminary year."
After conferring with the Reverend Gleason A. Reeder, pastor of his
church in Shelby, and after getting a promise of financial assistance
from his father, Williams decided to enroll in the University of Chicago's theology program. His motive for human service had been restored:

> With the help of my father's willingness to loan me the funds
> needed to offset the cost of postgraduate study for the ministry,
> my greatest requirement will be the knowledge of my fellow hu-
> mans, their motivating wants and aspirations, and how to be
> helpful to the solutions of their problems and the overcoming of
> the obstacles to their worthiest development . . . . With a head
> full of an exciting impression of a complex and super active
> world occupied by an amazingly diverse humanity, I registered at
> the Chicago Theological Seminary.[17]

The lure at the University of Chicago was the Social Gospel
clergyman, Graham Taylor. Taylor was well known for his work in
Christian sociology, especially in the Chicago area where he practiced
his own preachings by striving to improve social conditions through
work in his Chicago Commons Settlement House. It was Graham
Taylor and Charles R. Henderson, chaplain of the University of Chicago, who offered the first "social work" courses in Chicago. Williams
took courses with Taylor but also gained a wealth of practical experience by working in the settlement house. He reported "very little
social life" because of his classes plus the community welfare work he
was doing. The University of Chicago, resurrected by gifts from John
D. Rockefeller, measured its success by the number of souls it con-
verted to Christ.[18] Under the leadership of William Rainey Harper, it
communicated a strong sense of Christian mission similar to what
Williams had experienced at Oberlin. In those days, university presi-
dents still taught classes, and Williams studied Hebrew under Harper,
who gave "the ancient tongue . . . not only life but majestic life."[19]

In summarizing his year at the University of Chicago, Williams
found it "quite valuable and enjoyable under both the practical ap-
plier [that is, Graham Taylor] and the long trained analysts of the
prevailing Christian dogma [such as Harper]."[20] After his seminary

year at Chicago, Williams felt that he was ready for the ministry. He returned to Shelby in the summer of 1901 and talked with the family minister, Gleason A. Reeder, about how and where to obtain his first pastorate. Williams noted that "when he [Reeder] gave me an informal exam as to where my year of seminary had put me for Methodist Church service, he was, I fear, fairly shocked at the result. He proposed a year of serving two small churches that provided a 'horse and buggy plus $100 per month.'"[21] Williams sought further counsel with Dr. Ward Beecher Pickard, minister of the Epworth Methodist Church of Cleveland. Again, the news was less than encouraging. Dr. Pickard told Williams that he should start as an "itinerant minister," one who served smaller communities and filled in for other ministers as needs arose. Williams noted that both ministers felt that he "was not well prepared for a large church."

Williams's aspirations were for more than a "horse and buggy plus $100 per month" or some itinerant ministry. He left only a few clues about the dilemma these circumstances presented—he wanted the ministry, but his counselors felt that he should start lower on the ladder than he had expected. His father had been successful in business and his brother, Beatty, was doing well as an engineer in the Cooper-Bessemer Company in Mount Vernon, Ohio. Beatty had married Amy Fairchild, daughter of Cooper-Bessemer's president, but his talents were such that marrying the boss's daughter was not a prerequisite to his rise in the management hierarchy. Described as "highly intelligent, hard driving, and totally dedicated to the company's success," Beatty would serve as president of Cooper-Bessemer (now named Cooper Industries) from 1920 through 1940 and from 1941 through 1943.[22] Perhaps business would be the place for Whiting, who felt his "experience and training had revealed that the ministry lacked some of the desirable, worthwhile challenges of business."[23]

On the other hand, he felt that business lacked the idealism that he found so appealing in the ministry. Which path to choose? He was twenty-three years old and had no real responsibilities, so perhaps he simply needed experience, because he had found that "whenever there is a battle between logic and experience, experience is more likely to win."[24] People are shaped more by their experiences than by logic, he concluded, so who people are and what they become is largely the result of their experiences. So what he needed was more experience, and the best way to get this was to travel, see more, do more, and contemplate his future. He headed for Europe again, and fate would prevail over design in his life. While revisiting some favorite places, he encountered a group of Oberlin alumni who were touring under the auspices of the Oberlin College Travel Bureau. The tour director divulged to Williams that they were seeking someone who was an experienced traveler, spoke one or more foreign languages, and loved to travel. The job specification was perfect for Whiting Williams.

In Search of a Career

Whiting Williams was director of the Oberlin College Travel Bureau from 1901 through 1904. He arranged tours, handled finances, traveled abroad each year, and increased and improved his language skills. He conducted tours through such ancient sites as Karnak and Luxor in Egypt, Corfu and Piraeus in Greece, and Lima and Cuzco in Peru, and spent his evenings poring over the histories of these and other places. It was an exciting position, but hardly a career for an ambitious young man of his caliber. When his mentor, Henry C. King, became president of Oberlin College in 1903, new possibilities arose. King, a longtime faculty member and respected scholar, was expected to put Oberlin in step with the new century and the progressive changes that were becoming more evident across the country. The Social Gospel had supplanted Social Darwinism, and King was to lead Oberlin in this continuing crusade for social Christianity. The main problem facing Oberlin, the trustees felt, was a lack of finances, especially from private donors. King, however, was not a "promoter" nor did his training in philosophy and theology prepare him for the fund-raising task.[25]

Williams wrote to King in 1904, offering to serve Oberlin and King in whatever way possible. King's response was positive, and he offered Williams the position of assistant to the president with responsibility for administrative and financial matters. King noted the need to "reorganize the administrative forces" of Oberlin and offered Williams a salary of $2,500 per year.[26] In 1904, Williams began his work to raise money for Oberlin College and to be the external contact in financial matters where King felt poorly equipped to proceed.

Oberlin's financial situation, like most of America's private colleges, had never been overly abundant. Numerous private benefactors had supported the building program, the theological seminary, the library, and other endeavors. Oberlin had never resorted to the device of granting honorary doctorates as a means of providing recognition of famous individuals and perhaps also stimulating the loosening of some purse strings. An early historian of Oberlin noted that the college had "done little in the way of honorary degrees . . . [not because of] opposition to such degrees, only a traditional repugnance."[27] During a fund-raising drive, it was suggested that Orville and Wilbur Wright, two very famous Ohioans, be granted honorary doctorates. Neither Wilbur nor Orville had attended Oberlin, but their sister, Katherine, was an alumna. Furthermore, Katherine was vice-president of the class of 1899 when Whiting Williams was the senior class president. Whiting had "squired her about" and they became lifelong friends (she married Harry Haskell, also of the class of 1899, who became publisher of the *Kansas City Star*).

In discussing the Wright brothers, King noted to Whiting Williams that he was "having doubts about our plan to award honorary doctorates to the Wright brothers. I'm afraid we're doing this out of respect for Katherine. How do we protect ourselves from the charge that the Wright brothers were simply lucky high school boys?" Williams answered: "Oh no! They used very scientific methods from early on! I know because I was Katherine's escort to the Dayton Assembly Ball of Christmas, 1898. They [the Wright brothers] had an airplane wing mounted in a Uneeda cookie box glass door so they could watch tobacco smoke curl under and over the wing." King was impressed, admitting that this sounded "very scientific indeed. Let's go ahead with the doctorates."[28] After Williams's explanation that the Wright brothers were more than "lucky farm boys," and after the recommendation of King and approval by the trustees, Orville Wright and Wilbur Wright received their honorary LL.D.'s from Oberlin College in 1910.

Williams also found a new goal in life while he was King's assistant, that is, his "wish to train for a college presidency." He felt that the president's office gave him a perspective of top management in dealing with both internal and external matters. He advocated the use of more "science" in the study of students and curriculums and in improving the "commercial practices" of colleges.[29] Williams was successful in his role, but disillusionment began when he realized that only higher degrees and scholarship led to top administrative posts in colleges and universities. Williams had successfully completed his M.A. degree at Oberlin in 1909 but felt that his talents did not lie in being a scholar. After eight years as King's assistant, Williams felt that his goal of a college presidency was, like the ministry of a large church, unattainable.

A new path opened when Williams renewed his acquaintance

with an Oberlin College classmate, Al Fiebach, a Cleveland business-man. Fiebach told Williams that Cleveland's chamber of commerce needed help with its Committee on Benevolent Associations. The chamber of commerce had organized this committee in 1900 to inves-tigate and endorse worthy charities. The goal was to coordinate com-munity charity efforts, a rather innovative idea for the period.[30] Wil-liams, as we have seen, was strongly attracted to community welfare projects. His studies for the ministry at the University of Chicago and his work with Graham Taylor in the settlement house movement in Chicago were examples of his idea of the Social Gospel in action. Furthermore, Williams had gained experience in fund raising during the time he worked for King at Oberlin.

Williams was also attracted by the fact that Cleveland was the first city to attempt to bring all community charity into a planned group effort. Williams perceived that this "coordination of benevo-lence" would lead to "teamwork and efficiency" and open the door for givers of small and moderate means. One would not need wealth to be a philanthropist, and all persons could catch the spirit of giving, even on a modest income.[31] Williams assumed his duties at the Committee on Benevolent Associations in the fall of 1912. His leadership brought the association into the national limelight as an example of what could be done through organized community charity. The association was renamed the Cleveland Federation for Charity and Philanthropy in 1913, with Williams as its first executive director. Williams re-mained with the federation until 1916; he wrote, traveled, and helped to foster the notion of a community clearinghouse to promote charity and philanthropy. After three years as executive director, he felt that the federation needed new blood. He had taken the project from its committee stage full steam ahead into a federation of givers. This federation has been acclaimed as the forerunner of the modern com-munity chest association.[32]

Whiting Williams's life during this period had included more than just a search for a career. When he worked for King at Oberlin, Williams had shared an apartment near the campus with John Barber. In the fall of 1905 Williams had met an attractive new instructor of violin who had just joined the Oberlin faculty. The courtship must have been swift, for Barber recalled "the night in 1905 that you [Whit-ing] came in throwing your shoes at the ceiling after becoming engaged to a 'perfectly divine musician.' "[33] The divine musician's name was Caroline Harter, born May 11, 1878, in Canton, Ohio, to Isaac and Emma (Roberts) Harter. Caroline was an accomplished violinist and a graduate of the Geneva (Switzerland) Conservatory for Music. She taught for a while in 1905 at Wooster College in Wooster, Ohio.[34] Caroline Harter married Charles Whiting Williams on September 5, 1906, and their family grew with the birth of Carol Roberts (named after her maternal grandmother) Williams in 1908 and Harter Whiting Williams in 1914.

When Whiting Williams left the Cleveland Federation for Charity and Philanthropy in 1916, he was thirty-eight years old, with a wife and two young children, and had never really settled down for very long in what would be considered a career. His next job was selling group life insurance for the Equitable Life Assurance Company. Feeling that the wave of the future was group life insurance, an idea just developing at the time, Williams believed this was his chance to render "magnificent service" to those workers and members of society who could not afford individual life insurance policies. While selling insurance, he decided to drop "Charles" from his legal name because "Charles Williams" was so common.[35] The impact of this name change on his success as an insurance salesman is unknown, because yet another opportunity beckoned him to a new pasture. On one of his sales trips he stopped in Cleveland to sell a group insurance plan to the Hydraulic Pressed Steel Company. He evidently made quite a sales talk, for he was offered the job of vice-president and personnel director by J. H. "Mike" Foster, president of the company.[36] The position was newly created and the idea was that Williams would help the company deal with employee problems and meet employee needs.

Would life begin at forty for the "new" Whiting Williams? His long quest for a career was approaching its end. He had sought the ministry, traveled broadly, tried community fund raising, worked for Oberlin College's president, and sold life insurance. Now, at age forty, he accepted a new challenge, vice-president and personnel director for the Hydraulic Pressed Steel Company. He did not know it at the time, but this was the step that began the thousands of miles of journeys of the white collar hobo.

The Emergence of Personnel Work

Whiting Williams's newest opportunity in the personnel department of the Hydraulic Pressed Steel Company was in an emerging field that was striving to justify itself to corporate executives. The growth of the American economy in the nineteenth century had created unprecedented accumulations of human and physical resources in transportation and manufacturing organizations. A new nation just escaping the bonds of colonialism at the beginning of the nineteenth century, America had become a world industrial leader by the turn of the twentieth century. This rapid growth changed the means of production from small workshops and homes to factories where it was possible to manufacture products on a grand scale. This growth was accompanied by some costs — one of them being changing relations between managers and workers. When firms were smaller, those who owned the firm managed it as well. As Chandler has expressed so succinctly, "Owners managed and managers owned."[37] As these firms grew to a size where it was no longer possible for the owner-manager to keep in touch with all facets of the business, an intermediate level of management arose. These supervisors, and the middle-level managers, added later, served to coordinate lower-level activities and to provide information about performance to upper management. But organizational growth served to insulate employee relations from the personal touch of the owner-manager. The dilemma then was how depersonalization of labor-management relations could be made more employee-centered. One solution, which arose in the latter part of the nineteenth century, proposed "welfare" or "industrial betterment" schemes that would improve the conditions under which people labored. Companies such as National Cash Register, H. J. Heinz, Colorado Fuel and Iron, and International Harvester pioneered the establishment of welfare departments, which were supervised by a social secretary. The social secretary listened to and handled grievances, ran the sickroom of the workshop, provided for recreation and education, arranged transfers for dissatisfied workers, administered the dining facilities, prepared nutritious menus, and looked after the moral behavior of unmarried female factory employees.[38] The goal of these welfare departments was to improve the workers' lives, both on and off the job. Management believed that such a concern would lead to moral improvement and, eventually, to higher productivity.

A second branch of thinking about personnel also sought higher productivity, but the means to that end differed. Scientific management was a movement of the late nineteenth and early twentieth centuries that attempted to bring improved work methods and techniques to bear upon the problems of production. With Frederick Winslow Taylor as the polestar of this group, the answer to labor problems was sought not in labor but in management.[39] It was the responsibility of management to study work, to set fair standards, to improve work methods, to reduce fatigue, to provide incentives, and to find and train workers for their tasks. Those who followed scientific management saw in it betterment for all: higher wages and reduced fatigue for workers, lower costs and higher profits for management, and lower prices and more products for consumers. Joining the scientific management thinkers was a new breed of psychologists, including Hugo Munsterberg and Walter Dill Scott, who were concerned with applied industrial problems of vocational guidance, personnel testing, and improved personnel practices. Those who became employment managers or personnel directors were expected to advise line management on personnel selection, placement, orientation and training, wage payment plans, safety, and how to reduce labor turnover.

The object held in common by adherents of both the welfare approach and scientific management was the worker. The worker was not to be regarded as an inert instrument of production but as a vital resource whose circumstances could be improved for the benefit of both labor and management. A severe shortage of labor during World War I and the period immediately following caused a spurt of interest in personnel work. During the period from 1919 through 1920, as many personnel departments were created as had been organized in all years previous to that time.[40] For Hydraulic Steel, Whiting Williams's new employer, the role of personnel director was newly created and reflected the need to focus on improving relations between the company and its 3000 employees.

Until 1918, this emerging personnel task had been operated by most companies under various labels such as "labor," "welfare," "employment," and, of course, "personnel department." Williams perceived that these units were being added onto organizations largely as afterthoughts rather than being fully integrated into the central structure of management. Personnel looked after people, their hiring, training, pay, well-being, and a host of other items intended to develop and reward the best possible people for doing an organization's work. Williams's intent was that this attention to people be an organizationwide function rather than the province of personnel managers alone. Thus, personnel work was really dealing with human relationships. Due to the newness of personnel management, corporate executives failed to realize that the organization's relations with its workers were just as important as its relations with its customers, creditors, and other members of the community. Indeed, Williams deemed "the

worker . . . to be the veritable representative of the company itself"
as far as the public was concerned. By improving human relations
within the organization, all parties—workers, managers, and the
public—would benefit. There was no need for labor and management
to be antagonistic:

> The everlasting "scrapping" between Capital and Labor is now
> old stuff—out of date in a world which has paid millions of lives
> [i.e., World War I] to learn the lesson of genuine cooperation and
> teamwork. Good wages can be retained and national wealth in-
> creased only if manager and man and machine combine to pro-
> duce as never before. The price of maximum production is max-
> imum outlet for that human producer's best and biggest feelings.
> That in turn can be bought only with right relationships and
> associations with all the persons of the human producer's world.
> The coming together of factory management and factory man
> for the development of both will do more than humanize and
> justify this factory age.[41]

How could human relations be improved? How could "factory
management and factory man" be brought into the right relationship?
Williams admitted that he did not have the answers to those questions; indeed, the management of the Hydraulic Pressed Steel Company felt that Williams was not doing an adequate job as personnel
director. As Williams told the story,

> The first of my rather unusual efforts to understand the worker
> started when the president of the steel company for whom I was
> working called me in one day and said that he and his associates
> didn't think I was doing an adequate job of bridging the gap
> between the mind of management and the minds of the workers.
> He further intimated that unless early improvement could be
> made he would have to find some other man to tackle the job.
> Like anyone else under similar circumstances, I went home and
> proceeded to walk the floor for a few nights. As a result, I went
> in and asked him if he would give me a leave of absence for six
> months for the purpose of living the life of our workers.[42]

In later years, Williams explained that he realized the only way
he could improve as a personnel director was to "learn the other
fellow's point of view by sharing his experience; by walking in the
other fellow's moccasins," a new empathy could be gained.[43] Behind
Williams's conclusion that he needed to live the life of the worker was
another story—that of how people have typically sought to conduct
research into work and workers. Two methods seem to dominate the
research literature: (1) to interview the worker and record the impres-

sions; or (2) to administer a questionnaire and analyze the responses. Whiting Williams's method, however, was unusual: *become* a worker and be a participant-observer of work and workers. Perhaps the genesis of Williams's discovery of this device for probing the thoughts and feelings of workers was a thread within the Social Gospel that encouraged those who were concerned with existing conditions to do more than merely observe by becoming involved in daily life. We should recall the advice that John R. Commons gave as editor of the Oberlin student newspaper when he wrote that social Christians could increase their understanding by putting themselves "in the place of the working man" in order to know his problems by "personal contact."

Although Whiting Williams was not the first person to use the participant-observer method to study the lives of working people, his method did become unique when he used it repeatedly and systematically to study and improve upon labor-management relations. Others who preceded Williams as participant-observers of workers were more casual in their observations and did little with these discoveries once their initial curiosities were satisfied. In the summer of 1891, Walter A. Wyckoff, a graduate of the Princeton University class of 1888, struck out to "tramp" from Connecticut to California to learn how unskilled workers lived. After eighteen months and 2500 miles in such jobs as road builder, porter, farmhand, and logger, Wyckoff concluded that socialism would be a better economic system for unskilled workers because there would be less competition for jobs. After tramping from Connecticut to California, Wyckoff took a position at Princeton University teaching sociology and political economy.[44] The other participant-observer, Paul Goehre, was a theological student. He began his study in 1891 by taking a job in a machine-making factory in Chemnitz, Saxony (Germany). Goehre worked eleven hours a day and recorded the thoughts, feelings, and perceptions of the workers.[45] After three months as a worker, Goehre became a pastor, promoted consumer cooperatives, served in the Reichstag, and later became undersecretary of war in the Prussian cabinet.

Williams probably was unaware of the previous efforts of Wyckoff or Goehre, reaching his own decision while "walking the floor" and contemplating how best to understand the mind of the worker. After deciding, he did not go immediately to Foster but instead tried the idea out on one of his fellow executives, Henry Roemer, who remembered "with distinct clarity the time we sat at the lunch table and you disclosed your desire to learn to speak and more readily to understand the language of the working man. It was then that you told me of your intention to leave everything and start out on the road as a common laborer."[46] Williams then made his announcement to Foster. He would shed temporarily his white collar and become an itinerant laborer in order to find out what was on the worker's mind. Whiting Williams was ready for his double life.

TWO

The Double Life Begins

SO THE WHITE COLLAR executive had decided to become a hobo, to
travel from job to job, to stand in unemployment lines, and to rub
shoulders with the workers of America. Of course a few details had to
be arranged, such as providing for his family and disguising himself.
As Williams recalled:

> I made all my plans and took the train from Cleveland down to
> Pittsburgh in order to get a job in a steel plant, living the life of a
> steel plant laborer for the purpose of finding out, if possible,
> what makes him tick. I had changed my name [to Charlie Heit-
> man], put on some old clothes, left my razor at home for the
> moment, and put 25 dollars in my pocket on the understanding
> that if that 25 dollars were gone before I succeeded in getting a
> job as a common labourer it would be up to me to live at least six
> months the life of a jobless man.[1]

Hydraulic Steel's President Foster agreed to send Williams's pay-
check to Mrs. Williams each month. Foster did, however, have doubts
about Williams's ability to disguise himself sufficiently to gain the
workers' acceptance of him as a worker. Could this white collar man
pass himself off as a blue collar laborer? Would the lack of a tan or
the absence of calloused hands be an easy clue to the fact that he was
not accustomed to physical labor? What would the workers do if they
felt deceived? Undoubtedly, Williams must have asked himself these
same questions, but his experience proved the doubts unfounded:

> All my new companions accepted me so quickly and so com-
> pletely as the rough-neck and disreputable looking lowbrow that
> I pretended to be, that they positively hurt my feelings. . . . Only
> one man ever pierced through this rough disguise into the inner
> refinement of culture and ability of my college-bred soul. I have
> always felt that he wasn't playing quite fair, because at the mo-

20

ment he was very intoxicated: "There's something wrong here, stranger," [the intoxicated one said] "either you have committed some serious crime and are a fugitive from justice, or else a victim of some disgraceful secret sin, or you wouldn't be working in this forsaken town at $4 a day."[2]

This ready acceptance by the workers allowed Williams to take a big step, one that no other personnel manager had ever taken before—to live the life of the worker in order to assess the state of labor-management relations.

Labor-Management Relations in 1919

"Worse than at anytime in history," was Williams's assessment of the state of relations between labor, management, and the public in 1919.[3] To appreciate this conclusion it is necessary to examine the confluence of national and international events that provided the backdrop for Williams's travels and toils as an unskilled laborer. In 1917, the czar had been overthrown, and collectivism came by violent bloodshed to Russia. Subsequently, there had been communist uprisings in Bavaria and Hungary. The "Wobblies" (the Industrial Workers of the World) were provoking labor unrest, bomb-toting anarchists were allegedly lurking everywhere, and many Americans felt that the Bolsheviks were coming to overturn society.[4]

External events were only a part of the malaise that gripped America. Union leadership had become more aggressive, particularly in the hope of consolidating and enlarging the gains that organized labor had made during President Woodrow Wilson's administration. President Wilson's progressivism had created a favorable climate for labor to organize and bargain collectively. The Clayton Act (1914) removed from unions the onus of being "conspiracies in restraint of trade" as they had been labeled after the Sherman Antitrust Act (1890). Other prolabor legislation included the LaFollette Seamen's Act (1915) and the Adamson Act (1916), which established an eight-hour day for railroad operating employees.

Another event that roused the hopes of organized labor during the Wilson administration was the United States Commission on Industrial Relations, which investigated labor-management relations during the period from 1912 through 1915. Frank P. Walsh, a Wilson appointee, headed the commission, and Walsh was intent on proving the "callousness" of employers (especially John D. Rockefeller) and showing how they subdued labor.[5] President Woodrow Wilson promised labor that "there must be a genuine democratization of industry based upon a full recognition of the right of those who work . . . to participate in some organized way in every decision which directly affects their [the workers'] welfare."[6]

During World War I, the National War Labor Board (NWLB) also furthered many goals of organized labor. For example, the NWLB prohibited employers from antiunion activities; required time and one-half pay for work over eight hours per day; established the principle of shop committees elected by the employees to confer with management regarding grievances; proposed the principle of a "living wage" for all workers (in practice, this became an early minimum wage); acknowledged the right of women to receive "equal pay for equal work"; and provided mediation and conciliation services to settle disputes.[7]

The gains made under the Wilson administration promoted unionization of the work force and aroused new hope that more workers could be organized, especially in the industrial sector of the economy. Table 2.1 illustrates the growth in union membership during the period from 1914 through 1920. Almost 1.5 million workers were added to union rolls during the Wilson era and by 1920, membership had almost doubled. This drive to add members led to increased union militancy and more work stoppages. Table 2.2 indicates the shifts in the primary issues that led to work stoppages during this period. The year 1919 represented a postwar peak in work stoppages, with almost three times the number that had occurred in 1914. Union organization as the primary cause also peaked in 1919, with almost one-fourth of all work stoppages being caused by efforts to organize the unorganized.

The 3630 strikes in 1919 involved over 4 million workers. Early in the year a general strike took place in Seattle; later, the dormant Amalgamated Association of Iron, Steel, and Tin Workers of America awakened and lead a two-month strike of 300,000 steelworkers. The soft coal (bituminous) miners struck while the

TABLE 2.1. Union Membership: 1914–1920

Year	Union Members	Year	Union Members
1914	2,687,000	1918	3,467,000
1915	2,583,000	1919	4,125,000
1916	2,773,000	1920	5,048,000
1917	3,061,000		

Source: U.S. Bureau of the Census, *Historical Statistics of the United States: Colonial Times to 1970* (Washington, D.C.: U.S. Government Printing Office, 1975), pt. 1, p. 178.

steelworkers were out, and only the threat of an injunction kept the railroad brotherhoods from striking in support of the continued postwar federal operation of the railroads. Even the Boston police left their jobs in a protest of wages and working conditions.[8]

Labor had cause to strike with respect to pent-up demands for higher wages. To finance the war, government spending had increased; this stimulated the economy and led to inflation. Table 2.3 provides a measure of the rising cost of living between 1914 and 1920. By 1920, the cost of living had almost doubled, a fact that Williams would identify as one of the causes of industrial unrest among workers. While the cost of living increased, the government tried to keep a lid on wages, which led to a decline in real wages (see Table 2.4). In 1919, the dollar bought somewhat less than it had in 1913; and a desire for higher wages led to over 2000 work stoppages in 1919 (see Table 2.2). Not until 1920 would an upward trend in real wages be resumed.

TABLE 2.2. Work Stoppages and Their Causes: 1914–1920

Year	Total Stoppages	Wages and Hours		Union Organization		Other	
		Number	Percent of total	Number	Percent of total	Number	Percent of total
1914	1204	403	33	253	21	548	46
1915	1593	770	48	312	20	511	32
1916	3789	2036	54	721	19	1032	27
1917	4450	2268	51	799	18	1383	31
1918	3553	1869	56	584	17	900	27
1919	3630	2036	56	869	24	725	20
1920	3411	2038	60	622	18	751	22

Source: U.S. Bureau of the Census, *Historical Statistics,* p. 179. Causes of work stoppages are not always as clear-cut as these data suggest. The classification scheme used by the Bureau of Labor statistics emphasized primary causes.

TABLE 2.3. Consumer's Price Index: 1914–1920 (1967 = 100)

Year	Index	Year	Index
1914	30.1	1918	45.1
1915	30.4	1919	51.8
1916	32.7	1920	60.0
1917	38.4		

Source: U.S. Bureau of the Census, *Historical Statistics,* pp. 210-11.

TABLE 2.4. Real Wages: 1914–1920 (1913 = 100)

Year	Wage Index	Year	Wage Index
1914	99	1918	No data
1915	No data	1919	98
1916	No data	1920	112
1917	89		

Source: Donald L. Kemmerer and C. Clyde Jones, *American Economic History* (New York: McGraw-Hill, 1959), p. 531.

What's on the Worker's Mind?

It would not be hyperbole to say that the circumstances facing Williams when he left Cleveland for Pittsburgh were turbulent. As the data have indicated, workers were being caught in a situation of rising prices and lagging wages. Union leaders were seeking to preserve and advance the gains that labor had made in previous years. Strikes were frequent and sometimes bitter. Radicals sought to take advantage of the turmoil to advance their ideas about workers taking over the means of production, by violence if necessary. There were riots in Ireland, strikes in England and the United States, rebels in Romania, and Bolsheviks seemingly everywhere. Williams felt that some useful purpose would be served if he could uncover the problems. He felt that the only way to discover the causes of industrial unrest was to get "close" to the workers, because "men's actions spring from their feelings rather than their thoughts, and people cannot be interviewed for their feelings."[9]

What were the causes of industrial unrest? Were the workers being oppressed or exploited? Or were other factors contributing to poor labor-management relations? Williams felt that only a firsthand knowledge of the world of the worker would yield an answer. When he arrived in Pittsburgh, he had his first chance to stand at the gates of a steel mill and seek employment as an unskilled laborer. It was a common practice at this time for the foreman who needed a worker to do his own recruiting and selection. At American Rolling Mills, for example, "if a foreman was short of hands [workers] he went to the gate, looked over the crowd, picked out the man he wanted, and hired him."[10]

In Whiting Williams's first experience with this hiring scheme he reported the behavior of the job seekers when the foreman came out to scan the hopefuls at the gate: "We all bunched up our shoulders so as to look husky and tried to catch his eye." After three days of frustrations, and just as Williams's cache of twenty-five dollars was about to run out, he got a job in the "cinder pit" gang of a steel mill, cleaning out the cooling open hearth furnaces so they could be re-bricked and refired. Williams, in describing his introduction to the world of the unskilled laborer, wrote that:

> we began at five-thirty [p.m.] — three of us Americans, one Italian boy, one Mexican, one Greek, and several Slavic and Russian fellows — all of them hardly able to say more than a very few English words, though they had all been in this country a number

of years. It was bricks and brick-bats, and then more bricks and
more "bats." We shovelled or pitched broken bricks into big ladles or boxes in the "cinder-pit" beneath us at the back of the
furnace; we piled good ones; we took turns getting into the hot
ruins of the furnace substructure and lifted and tossed and shovelled them up to the platform for the others to carry and shovel.
Occasionally we rested a few moments. At all times we sweat —
especially when down in the ruins.[11]

It was hot, dirty work, the shifts were twelve hours long, and the
pay was forty-five cents per hour with time and one-half pay for
hours over eight. This meant that a worker earned $6.30 for the
twelve-hour "turn." In his diary for February 5, 1919, Williams
described a typical day in the cinder pit:

Too dog-tired for pushing a train of thought with a pen. Here's
why:

Midnight. — Eating a good lunch packed by my new landlady
(seven dollars the week) while seated up by the warm "slag-vent"
at the back of a hot furnace after shovelling, throwing, and
carrying brick-bats and hard "cinder" out of the bottom of our
same old torn-down No. 13, steadily from 5:30.

12:30 A.M. — Back to the shovel and cinder, and aching, shovel-
worn forearms.

2:30. — Constant shovelling, always within a few feet of a noisy
chisel eternally put-put-ing like a machine gun, chattering and
biting and scolding at the adamantine "cinder." (Taught how to
operate it — very heavy, hard, jumpy work — by a negro and a
friendly Spaniard.) Sorer forearms. Less supervision — boss reported asleep.

Wonderful views of pourings across the cinder-pit, upturned
empty ladles soaring back to their stands, like views of heaven
for beauty (too tired to describe now); dragon-like "mixer" which
tilts its mouth and its hulk to receive or give out its 250 tons of
yellow hot iron; glorious graphite sparklets poured from small
ladle, which goes from the mixer to the fronts of the furnaces to
give the drink of hot "pig" as needed for the steel.

Less shovellings, more carryings and throwings — wrists too tired
for shovelling; head thumping from that eternal machine gun of
a drill.

4:00 o'clock. — Thank God! Only one hour more!

5:00. — Everybody swears, quits, sighs for six.

5:55. — Shovel shanty — shovels deposited. Wait for whistle
around small stove — everybody silent, groggy, heads on hands.
Bosses loud in Slavic mixed with American profanity.

6:00. — Ah! — whistle at last! Everybody jumps and wearily starts
home through the dark and snow.

6:45. — Bath finished. (Thank the Lord for hot water!) Go for
sausage and cakes.

7:45. — Into bed. (Thank the Lord also for clean sheets!)

3:30. — Awake. Go to work? All in favor — ? Wrists vote "No."
Neck and shoulders vote "No." Compromise arranged — more
sleep.

4:15. — Write diary in bed.

4:45. — (Three minutes from now) get up, put on dirty clothes
laid off only a few minutes on other side of that blessed sleep.
Boarding-house, supper, package lunch, and —

5:30. — Show number check to gate policeman, report to labor
shanty and repeat as before till midnight.[12]

Williams's first excursion into the world of the worker lasted for
seven months and placed him in a variety of jobs (see Table 2.5). The
significance of Williams's contributions to understanding industrial
conditions and labor-management relations resides not in the jobs he
held, but in the insights he gleaned from his observation of and participation in the worker's domain. From his experiences he formulated five general factors that facilitated an understanding of workers:
(1) the importance of the job in terms of worker status and self-
respect; (2) the results of unemployment and insecurity; (3) the impact
of fatigue and working conditions; (4) the role of pay in worker
motivation; and (5) the relationship between the worker and management, especially the first-line supervisor. Worker dissatisfaction with
any of these factors could cause industrial unrest.

The Worker's Prayer

As an inside observer, Williams was able to assess the workers'
feelings about many things; and the one item he found to be paramount was simply the importance of having a job. The worker's

TABLE 2.5.   Whiting Williams's Jobs: February–August 1919

Industry	Length of Stay (approximate)	Job Title	Duties
Steel	One month	Cinder pit gang/ Millwright's helper	Cleaned out cold furnaces for re-bricking/promoted to assist millwright.
	One month	Catcher's helper	Used tongs to catch hot sheets of steel after they were rolled.
	Two weeks	Hooker	Attached crane chain to piles of steel sheets.
Coal	One month	Loader	Shoveled loosened coal into cars for transport to surface.
	One month	Millwright's helper	Helped shore up tunnels.
Railroad	One week	Machinist's helper	Did repair work in the "round house."
Shipbuilding	Three weeks	Reamer's helper	Helped prepare holes for riveters.
	Two weeks	Reamer	Prepared holes for riveters.
Iron ranges	One week	Unable to find employment	
Oil refining	Three weeks	Dock helper	Stenciled barrels of petroleum by-products.

prayer was "Give us this day our daily job" because a job meant "bread," sustenance for the worker and his or her family.[13] Williams had no manual skills so he ended up with unskilled jobs, which he found were largely staffed by immigrants: Russians, Croatians, Italians, Greeks, Poles, Mexicans, and Slavs. As a white American, Williams was suspect. One of his fellow workers commented that "no white American work in steel-plant labor gang unless he's nuts or booze-fighter."[14] Williams's experience in the Oberlin College Travel Bureau came in handy, however, and he found that his smattering of Spanish, Italian, French, and German helped to allay the workers' suspicions.

Williams's experiences with standing in line to get a job appear to have been caused primarily by the fact that he was looking for unskilled positions. Most of the unemployment in 1919 was caused by the postwar release of military personnel into the civilian labor force, and it remained confined largely to jobs for unskilled workers. In Pittsburgh, Williams noted, there were 12,000 unskilled laborers looking for work; yet there was a shortage of 1700 miners. Today we would call this problem "structural unemployment," a situation involving plentiful jobs for those with the right skills existing simultaneously with unemployment for those who lack the skills required by the labor market.

The daily prayer for a job, however, should not be viewed as the sole province of the unskilled worker. One of the many perceptive insights that Williams gained was that all persons—including managers and executives—measured their individual worth and their value to society in terms of their jobs. The main difference between those at the bottom of the job hierarchy and those at the top was any particular individual's ability to control his or her employment opportunity. An unskilled person had less opportunity to control the employment situation than a more skilled, better trained, or more highly educated individual. "The worker lives and moves and has his being on the job," said Williams, meaning that the job influenced social standing, and that how a person earned a living influenced where and how that person and his or her family lived their lives.[15] Furthermore, without a job, a person was isolated not only economically but also from the community and society: "[the worker's] vision of himself, his friends, his employer, and the whole of this world to come is circumscribed by his job."[16] This made a person's job central to his or her lifestyle, friends, place of residence, pursuit of leisure, and self-esteem.

To illustrate how feelings of self-worth were based upon what a person did, Williams often told the story of how he learned the difference between a hobo, a tramp, and a bum. The story began when Williams erred by suggesting to an unshaven, unsavory character that hoboes, tramps, and bums were all of the same breed. The unshaven one replied:

> Say, you don't suppose I'd be a tramp, do you? But do you know that this country couldn't exist without us 'boes! The Northwest's gotta have us guys work at lumber in the winter and then Oklahoma's gotta have us work in wheat in summer, and we gotta make quick connections, too, or the crop spoils. So we gotta take the train and we don't believe in spendin' money on fares. But a tramp!—Huh! He just *walks* from job to job because he don't care whether he ever gets there or not—and nobody else does, neither. A bum—well, he's no good whatever. He just bums a drink or a sandwich off people from day to day, 'thout doin' nothin' worth while for it. A tramp is miles above a bum.[17]

Within factories, Williams observed a job hierarchy whose operations had little or nothing to do with pay. He often illustrated this by telling the story of his promotion from the cinder pit gang to a millwright's helper in the steel mill. His pay was two cents per hour more, which was not much, but one of his former fellow shovelers commented: "Hey, buddy, where you catchem job, huh? Millwright gang, oil can, wrench, and no more goddam shovel. My God, you are a lucky son of a gun."[18] Williams's promotion moved him up on the job hierarchy, not because of the two cents per hour raise, but because the nature of his job had changed from the dirty, hot work of a shoveler to the assistant of a skilled worker with a cleaner, more pleasant job.

Prior to Williams, scant attention had been paid to the social, as well as the job, organization in the workplace. People brought their feelings to work, however, and they took them home. By his observations, Williams was able to bring attention to the job and the workplace in terms of their influence on how people felt about themselves. Jobs carried a social, as well as an economic, meaning. Workers might pray for a daily job to earn their bread, but they also compared jobs, ranked them to determine their group standing, and derived their self-respect and respect for others from what they did. At the time, these were unique insights.

Job Scarcity and the Worker

Although unemployment in 1919 averaged only 1.4 percent of the total work force on an annual adjusted basis, the return of numerous military personnel to civilian jobs caused some job insecurity, especially among lesser-skilled employees. Since workers perceived their jobs as a central component of their physical and social well-being, the lack of a job, conversely, became one of life's traumatic events. Three outcomes were possible, Williams felt, if workers were frustrated in their attempts to find a job or to find the right job: (1) the workers would listen to those who proposed radical solutions; (2) they would form unions; and/or (3) they would restrict output.

One of Williams's interests, quite possibly because of public attention to the subject at the time, was that of "radicals," most notably the "Bolshes" (Bolsheviks) and the "Wobblies" (the Industrial Workers of the World—IWW). After attending meetings where radical speakers agitated the workers by promising jobs for all, Williams noted that the workers were skeptical. Williams felt that management, by neglecting to communicate with workers about "[its] plans

and purposes, the aims and ideals—the character" of the company,
played into the hands of the radicals.[19] Workers, not hearing the position of management, listened to those who did offer something attractive for them. Furthermore, adverse actions without explanations by
management could also drive workers to seek radical solutions. Williams quoted one worker who had been through such a bitter experience: "Eight year I work in plant in New York, after coming to this
country. What he [the supervisor] want I do. I work all the time and
all the time happy. But one day the boss come down mad, and he say
'you fired,' and for eight year I been Bolshevik."[20] Poor communication, arbitrary actions by management, and the lack of a job provided
opportunities for radicals to gain a foothold. Otherwise, Williams
dismissed the radicals as a source of danger. Workers who had jobs
paid no attention to them and the other workers were skeptical. If
jobs were available, Williams felt, the radicals would have no appeal.
The workers were not alienated from society, as some would maintain, but desired to be a part of the social mainstream through their
jobs and the opportunities they presented.

Unions, in Whiting Williams's mind, were not radical. On June
15, 1919, Williams attended the annual convention of the American
Federation of Labor (AFL) in Atlantic City, New Jersey. There he met
Samuel Gompers, president of the AFL, as well as other labor leaders
including John P. Frey of the iron molders, Matthew Woll of the
photo engravers, and William Green of the coal miners. Williams
noted that the "radicals from the west" (meaning those of the IWW
and the Bolsheviks) tried to take over the convention but that they
were "put down" by the responsible leaders of labor. Of paramount
interest at this convention was the role of "industrial" unions (that is,
a union formed by industry regardless of skill categories) versus the
traditional "craft" make-up of the AFL. Because of the favorable
climate for union organizing, the AFL was trying to organize the steel
industry, and much of the convention discussion concerned the best
strategy for the organizing drive.

Unions, in Williams's view, were a result of the worker's search
for job security:

> The understanding of the importance of the daily job helps also
> to an understanding of the labor union. In addition to its more
> public appearances on behalf of better wages and hours, the
> union is likely to be quietly busy helping to find work for its
> members and then to protect them against unjust firing. It is

impossible to help wondering if the unions would have grown to anything like their present size if all the managers felt more keenly how seriously this problem of the daily job touches the life and soul of the worker.[21]

The appeal of the union to the needs of the worker for job security distinguished the responsible union leadership from the irresponsible; Gompers and others were willing to work within the economic and political system to help the worker, while the radicals sought to overthrow the system.

By focusing on job security, Williams had anticipated one of the major theories regarding why unions form. It is not possible to examine here all interpretations of labor union formation, but one widely accepted approach has been the "job consciousness" theory of Selig Perlman. Perlman proposed that workers perceived a scarcity of job opportunities and formed unions in order to control this scarce opportunity by restricting access to a job (for example, by restricting the number of apprentices); developing rules about who would do the work (jurisdictions); making rules about how the job would be done (work methods rules); and forming a "common rule" to provide against unjust dismissals and to govern worker conduct to preserve union solidarity.[22] This job consciousness distinguished unions in the United States from the radical reform unions of Great Britain and Europe. The successful unions in America in the nineteenth century were those that were job-oriented rather than reform-bent. Williams's observations anticipated Perlman's conclusion that unions succeeded because they appealed to a central need of the workers: the job.

Restriction of output was another device workers used for coping with job insecurity. Williams's observation of the phenomenon of restriction of output was by no means new. Frederick W. Taylor, of scientific management fame, had called this "soldiering" and he found two types: "natural," or the inclination of workers to relax their pace, and "systematic," or restriction caused by peer pressures to avoid producing too much work and including the notion that one worker could harm him or herself or other workers by doing more than his or her share. Williams explained how this "lump of labor" notion worked and why it caused workers to restrict output:

> It is hard to blame a man for not keeping a close eye upon the pile of rough material that means his job, as he sees that pile getting smaller, and the pile of finished material growing larger and larger. It is hard for that man not to go slow, when he

realizes that at five o'clock when the whistle blows, the boss may come to him and say: "Joe, this will get you your time. Won't need you in the morning. Ye see, th' work's all done."[23]

Fatigue and group norms also influenced the workers' behavior. In his very first job in the cinder pit, Williams experienced both of these factors:

When I started in I figured I'd keep going as long as I could and loaf after I was played out. I couldn't get on with the program. First the little Italian boy tapped me on the shoulder and advised "Lotsa time! Take easy!" I slowed down a notch or two. A little later the Russian, wiping off the sweat as he sat for a moment on a pile of bricks, cautioned: "You keel yourself. Twelve hours long time." Finally, after every one had remonstrated, I got down to a proper gait—so you'd have to sight by a post to see if I was moving. But at that I guess they knew better than I—I'm certainly tired enough as it is.[24]

Williams introduced a colorful phrase to explain restriction of output, or "stringing out the job:"

One look at the world through the [worker's] eyes given by this daily need of work makes it immensely easier to understand the worker's attitude toward the restriction of output—stringing out the job. Whether we like it or not, even a short experience will convince anyone that the worker has considerable right to fear, as a practical, day-by-day proposition, that by working too hard or too well he may work himself out of his job—that by producing too much he may produce himself out of that indispensable daily bread.[25]

For the same reasons, one could explain the worker's fear of technological advancements. The very thought of being out of work was enough to make the worker "feel highly doubtful about the introduction of machinery—very hesitant to accept the calm assurance of the economists that he should have no fear because the whole thing is bound to work out in the long run through the increased production and the resultant cheapening of goods."[26] On every job Williams reported that the workers told him, "Psst! Buddee, psst! Take it easy. Go slow! Don't keel yourself! Lotsa time."[27]

Management contributed to the worker's perception of job scarcity. Some employers hired and then laid off workers when the work slackened. For example, Williams worked in a mine where the miners faced a great uncertainty about the next day's work. At quitting time each day, the next day's plans could be determined by listening to the whistle—three blasts on the whistle meant "work tomorrow," while two blasts signaled no work. Under these circumstances, workers tended to "string out the job," hoping to extend the employment period. Williams noted that some companies had made the decision to regularize production. This meant that the ups and downs of a seasonal cycle (as in the coal industry) would be smoothed out by producing for inventory during slack times. This production planning by management would be more costly because of inventory carrying costs, but those costs would be offset by less restriction of output. Williams felt that labor and management could find a mutual interest in steady production, which led to a steady job.

In summary, the job was all-important to the worker. The job was more than bread and butter, and its nature affected the worker's concept of self, family, and community status. Unions would succeed if they met the worker's need for job security. Management, too, should not neglect this need but should speak of its own "plans and ideals" and should regularize production.

Tiredness and Temper

It was Williams's habit to record his experiences in a diary each evening while the day's events were still fresh in his mind. One entry, made while working in a steel mill, spoke volumes: "Too tired to write tonight." "Tiredness and Temper," or "T 'n T," was Whiting Williams's way of expressing the explosive effect of long hours of work and fatigue as causes of industrial problems. The industry that made the greatest impact on this thinking was steel, where the "turns" (shifts) were predominantly twelve hours in length, six days a week, with an occasional "long turn" when a worker had to work a Sunday shift.

The length of the workday in American industry had been an issue for some time. Coal miners had been on an eight-hour day since 1897 and the United States Industrial Commission of 1898 had proposed similar hours for industry in general. Goldmark, in her study of fatigue, concluded that the United States lagged behind Great Britain and most European countries in reducing hours of work. The United States, she maintained, could shorten the workday and maintain the same (or greater) total output level, because workers would be less fatigued and more efficient. Wages would decline temporarily, but would be regained as added efficiency brought wages back up.[28] During World War I, the National War Labor Board had not specified the length of the workday, but decreed that any work over eight hours per day must be paid at a wage rate of one and one-half times the normal wage rate.

Opponents of the shorter workday maintained that workers were lazy and merely wanted to do less work. Some forty years later, Douglas McGregor would become famous for developing what he called Theory X and Theory Y. Theory X represented, in McGregor's opinion, the traditional view of human nature, which operated on the premise that "the average human being has an inherent dislike of work and will avoid it if he can." McGregor went on to reject this view and formulated, instead, Theory Y, which was based on the assumption that "the average human being does not inherently dislike work."[29] Williams's answer to the opponents of the shorter workday sounds very much like what Douglas McGregor would call Theory Y. It was Williams's view that "we malign human nature when, in seeking a way out into a new Utopia, we presume that the average human being does not wish to work. Men do want a chance to work. We make a tremendous mistake when we interpret the first sign of a demand for shorter hours in terms of laziness."[30]

Williams perceived that many human relations problems were connected with long hours of work: fatigue for both workers and supervisors; lowered productivity; and worsened interpersonal relations both on the job and at home. Hours of work varied by industry, and Williams found different hours prevailing for different types of skills. For example, the "rollers" in the steel mills worked eight-hour shifts while the unskilled workers worked twelve. In some steel companies the eight-hour shift was in effect for all workers, just as it was on the railroads and at the coal mines.

With respect to working conditions in general, Williams found them good. Although the coal mines were cramped and dirty, mine safety was foremost and daily inspections were conducted to detect gas leaks, determine the soundness of the timber shoring, and detect faults in the seams, which could cause a collapse. Frequent state inspections reinforced management's emphasis on safety. At the coal mines Williams also found decent houses provided or subsidized by the company, hot showers, clinics, nurses, baby clinics, schools for both day and night classes, electric lights, a library, and other amenities that offset some of the hardships. Williams also recorded the view that workers liked "smoky" towns because smoke meant there was work to be obtained there. Steel mills were hot and dangerous, and

Williams felt that a good pair of gloves and paying attention to one's job were essential to keeping one's body intact.

In brief, fatigue—T 'n T—caused by long hours of work appears to have been a main concern of the workers. Williams was a firm believer in shorter hours of work, not just to reduce fatigue but also to improve interpersonal relations. Williams would continue to promote the abolition of the twelve-hour shift in steel and the importance of shorter working hours to defuse T 'n T.

"Wages are Interesting, But . . ."

It was popular during this period to take the position that people were primarily motivated by money—the "economic man" concept. The offering of incentives for greater output, typically called piecework or payment by results, was an ancient practice which antedated the Industrial Revolution. Whiting Williams was skeptical about the efficacy of the idea that people would work harder if they were given more money, admonishing that "we give the dollar altogether too great an importance when we consider it the cause of men's industry. . . . The dollar is merely an especially convenient and simple means for facilitating the measurement of a man's distance from the cipher of insignificance among his fellows. . . . Beyond a certain point, the increase of wages is quite as likely to lessen as to increase effort."[31] Williams's view was unique in that he established money as a means of social comparison. The pay one received was not considered in absolute terms, but in relation to what others were receiving. Our "distance from the cipher of insignificance" among our fellowmen was facilitated by using the dollar as a unit of account for measurement. This did not mean that money was not important, but that it was a carrier of social value that might enhance, or deflate, how we viewed ourselves relative to others.

This conclusion set Whiting Williams apart from others of this time who speculated about people's motives. One popular viewpoint was that "instincts" determined our behavior; thus, we acted to pursue instincts of workmanship, sex, curiosity, self-assertion, possession, and so on.[32] According to Williams, we were not motivated by instincts, but by the "desire to be someone, to gain self respect."[33]

Another interesting conclusion concerned Williams's observation that some workers chose *not* to work when they felt that they had earned enough. Workers had some mental image of how much was "enough" and then chose leisure time rather than more hours of work. Williams did not use special terminology for this phenomenon, but what he observed is what labor economists now call a backward-bending supply curve of labor. In Williams's time, the prevailing position of economic analysis assumed that the higher the wages the more willing people were to work. Williams observed, however, that workers would choose to substitute leisure for work once some magic wage level had been reached. The absolute amount of wages at which one would substitute leisure for work would vary, of course, for each individual according to his or her desired standard of living. The interesting thing is that Williams observed this phenomenon in practice before it found articulation as economic theory.

Economists of the mercantilist school of economic thought in the seventeenth and eighteenth centuries believed that income and the supply of labor were negatively related—that is, that as wages rose, less labor would be forthcoming. Nineteenth-century theorists, particularly Alfred Marshall, took the position that higher wages led to more labor, because people wished to maximize their income (that is, labor supply and wages were positively related). This nineteenth-century view prevailed until the 1930s when empirical studies began to show that the mercantilists (and Whiting Williams) were right—income and the amount of labor supplied were negatively related.[34] The wheel of history had come full circle.

Williams's conclusion that "wages are interesting, but the *job* is the axis on which the whole world turns for the working man" ran counter to the conventional wisdom of the time.[35] Of course, there would be no wages without a job, but Williams was saying more than that. The animating drive was that of self-respect, to stand in the eyes of others as a worthwhile person. The job was the main determinant of that, and money was the measuring stick for making comparisons. Pay was important, but only as a measure of a person's standing in some relevant reference group. Thus, when workers complained of the "HCL," Williams's shorthand for the high cost of living, their complaint was that they were losing standing in relation to whatever their social and economic benchmark was.

The Eleventh Commandment

Williams learned that the only thing that exceeded a worker's ignorance of his or her employer was the employer's ignorance of his or her employee. The barrier between labor and management, which Williams called the "Chinese Wall" (presumably the Great Wall of China), was "mutual suspicion," which fostered mutual ignorance. The cause of this wall was traced by Williams to the foreman, the first-line supervisor immediately above the operative workers in the organizational hierarchy. The foreman, to the workers, *was* management, for he or she was typically the only manager with whom they ever dealt. As Williams expressed it: "The foreman certainly is the holder of the worker's life and future, and he certainly is — in most of the places I've been — far from being what he should be in the world that has been made safe for democracy."[36]

Some of the bad qualities that Williams found in foremen were the habits of saying "hey you" rather than learning a person's name and ignoring or being indifferent to their workers. One worker's advice to Williams regarding how to handle a "yeller" (a yelling foreman) was to "always save yerself and go as easy as ye can, but allus keep yer eye peeled, and know where the boss is. And when he's comin' your way, work like the devil!"[37]

Williams found that the foremen were generally not educated, nor were they trained in how to manage workers. For the most part, the foremen "rose through the ranks," having been especially good workers whom management then tapped for supervisory positions. One solution to this problem was training for foremen, because Williams felt that "every company is known by the management it keeps."[38] At the hub of this training for foremen should be the lesson to treat people with decency so they could maintain their self-respect, for as one worker explained: "How men like [their] foreman, that depends on hees character. Me, I do best for heem who [is a] gentleman and treats me like [a] gentleman."[39]

Williams noted that workers would be more productive if their foremen relied on "leadership, head-work, and skill" rather than on "proddings and strong, super-heated language." This new way of relating manager to worker was capsulized by Williams's "Eleventh Commandment": Thou shalt not take thy neighbor for granted. Managers needed to get to know their workers and to treat them decently.

Another suggestion for improving labor-management relations was to improve communications. This idea had two separate but related facets: on the one hand, management needed to explain better how the workers' efforts fitted into the total scheme of things; and on the other hand, management needed to listen better. In terms of telling the workers about the company, management needed to help workers relate their efforts to the company and the community. An explanation of why the company did something enabled the workers to see the results of their efforts in terms of serving others. The idea of improved listening skills for managers enabled Williams to begin his thinking about worker participation in the company. These ideas eventually became part of the "work simplification movement," in which people were asked to "work smarter, not harder." Williams's experiences confirmed that workers had ideas that management was not using. He summarized his observations in this fashion: "If I [Whiting Williams] ever run across a foreman who asks me if my doing of the job gives me any hunches that would save other men's labor, or the company money, and then nods his head and thanks me for the suggestion—well, the shock will probably be fatal."[40]

In brief, management did not tap the brains of those who did the work so that their improvements could be instituted. Management and labor too often took each other for granted rather than seeking their mutual interests. Through better supervision, labor-management relations could be improved.

Back to Cleveland

On September 9, 1919, "Charlie Heitman" became Whiting Williams once more. He had spent over seven months loading coal cars, handling hot rolled steel, shoveling out cinder pits, and working on various other jobs. He recorded in his diary his impressions of the people he had worked with, their hopes and fears, and what it was like to be a worker. Summing up his feelings, Williams noted that "the most outstanding impression of all is that I found my companions in the labor gangs so completely human and so surprisingly normal. It makes me smile at myself now as I recall the air of mystery and 'differentness' with which my mind had surrounded all these workers back there in the days before I started out to join them."[41]

With the barriers of white collar–blue collar division removed, he found that workers were more like than unlike the rest of us. With this fundamental sameness, the idea of a "working class" made little sense. Williams mused that "white collars are nice, but I hate to think of all the interesting people I've evidently been missing because of [a white collar]."[42] The white collar hobo had learned what he felt he needed to know to become a better director of personnel. When he shaved off the mustache of Charlie Heitman and resumed his white collar ways, he did not yet realize what his travels would bring.

THREE

The Hobo Goes Abroad

WHITING WILLIAMS'S return to Cleveland brought about the demise of "Charlie Heitman," but only for a short time. The original plan had been for the vice-president and personnel director of the Hydraulic Pressed Steel Company to take a short leave to find out what was on the worker's mind. The scenario was supposed to read: white collar to itinerant laborer and back to white collar—but that was not to be. After Williams presented his report, the company executives suggested that he speak before the Cleveland chamber of commerce. Then, the Chicago chamber of commerce asked to hear Williams's report; and then, *Collier's* magazine wrote to request a series of articles about his experiences. As Williams explained, "So much attention was given to my report—almost as if I had come as a man from Mars—that I resigned and devoted myself for some years to that particular kind of study."[1]

"Charlie Heitman" would rise again to study conflict in the steel, railroad, and coal industries. He would travel abroad to study the worker in England, Wales, Scotland, France, Germany, the USSR, and other places. The results of these travels would become the books and articles that Charlie's alter ego, Whiting Williams, wrote and the reports he prepared for those who solicited his advice on the status of the worker in industry. At the age of forty-two, Whiting Williams had found a new career.

The Steel Strike of 1919

Williams's immediate concern upon his return to Cleveland was the threat of a nationwide strike in the steel industry. He had spent a large portion of his time as an itinerant laborer in that industry, and he wanted to share his experiences with labor, management, and the public with the hope that a speedy resolution of the dispute could be reached and a strike avoided.

The end of the shooting war in Europe had marked the beginning of organized labor's struggle to solidify and enlarge its wartime gains. Employers, on the other hand, saw the end of the war as a means of rolling back the unions' advances. At no place in American industry was the desire to restore the "open shop" of worker choice in unionization more fervent than it was in the steel industry. From labor's viewpoint, however, steel was a major industry which had long been a target of union-organizing efforts and which also could provide labor with an entrée into other industries. Skilled ironworkers had organized in 1876 as the Amalgamated Association of Iron, Steel, and Tin Workers of America, which by 1891 enjoyed 24,068 members and a position as the strongest trade union of that period.[2] In a strike and confrontation with the Carnegie Steel Company at Homestead, Pennsylvania, in 1882, the ironworkers lost a battle, however, and the union fell into decline. Union interest in organizing the steel industry was revived, however, after the gains made during the reign of the National War Labor Board. In 1918, under the leadership of Samuel Gompers, the American Federation of Labor (AFL) president, a committee from twenty-four craft unions was formed in an effort to organize the steel industry. When Whiting Williams attended the AFL convention in 1919, committee secretary William Z. Foster reported that 100,000 workers had been organized. "They call me a radical," Foster told Williams,

> but I'm only anxious to get somewhere; while all the old fellows say: "Oh, yes, we've tried to get the big plants too many times already!" Why, if we could only get the heads of these other twenty-four internationals anxious — genuinely interested — we'd have the whole industry in a month! . . . Of course, where the men have right wages, hours, working conditions, treatment, and all that, and are happy, we ain't got a chance with 'em.[3]

Williams concluded that Foster was "a very quiet fellow of the intellectual type, partly red-haired, mainly bald — not much magnetism, and, I judge, a poor speaker."[4] Others did judge Foster a radical, but at this point Williams reserved judgment on his motives.

In 1919, the National Committee for Organizing Iron and Steel Workers flexed its muscles and at least 350,000 workers went on strike on September 22. Because Williams had perspired in the cinder pit gang, handled hot, rolled steel, and worked side by side with those who were on strike, he felt he had some insights into the reasons behind the dispute. Just six weeks after Williams had left Cleveland, and while employed in the United States Steel Corporation's Homestead, Pennsylvania, plant, he had written that: "Carnegie Steel [*sic*] is losing money in large sums because it thinks labor is a commodity and a *cheap* one."[5] He also noted that the company was failing to give "recognition and satisfactions that touch his [the worker's] spirit and feelings and attitudes." Steel company management "kidded itself" when it thought that by hiring a worker, it also bought the worker's "want to" and "know how to." Williams had ample experiences as a steelworker to confirm his observations that workers were tired and poorly motivated and that foremen were "drivers" and ill-tempered due to long hours of work. "If business is to succeed," he wrote, "it must build on human beings because success in our relations with others is paramount to our success in business." He mentioned meeting his old friend from Oberlin, John R. Commons, at the AFL convention, and he quoted Commons as saying that "capitalism gave men security—not simply security of property but of life, liberty, and the pursuit of happiness."[6]

Without a belief in these human values, industrial unrest was sure to occur. In Williams's diary entry of August 25, 1919, he had noted that a strike was brewing. He also noted the causes as poor worker-manager relations; the lack of a "normal" life because of twelve-hour shifts and six- (sometimes seven-) day workweeks; "chronic fatigue"; and the high cost of living. It was shown earlier (see Tables 2.3 and 2.4) how inflation in the postwar period had contributed to declining real wages. The common wage for unskilled workers in the steel industry was forty-five cents per hour, plus time and one-half pay for more than eight hours of work per day. This wage was two cents per hour below the average hourly earnings of workers in manufacturing in 1919. Unrest, then, was due not only to the lower than average wages, but also to the rising cost of living.

In anticipation of labor militancy, U.S. Steel's President Elbert H. Gary told his top executives to "keep ahead of trouble" by making "sure we are liberal in the protection of our workmen and their families. Make the Steel Corporation a good place for them to work and live. Don't let the families go hungry or cold. . . . Take care of your men. It will cost some money but I do not think that this is very important. [Leave] no just ground for criticism on the part of those who are connected with the movement of unrest."[7]

Although this was a worthy policy regarding labor-management relations, Williams felt that no policy could be better than the abilities of those who were called upon to implement it. The weak link in labor-management relations at U.S. Steel were those first-line supervisors who represented management to the worker. Williams had observed that many of them were poorly trained, inept in human skills, and, as he called them, "drivers," "riders," and "rawhiders."[8] Gary's policies regarding the treatment of workers would be of little value if they were implemented ultimately by that type of foreman. Williams wrote to Gary that he needed to project his desire to improve worker-management relations down to the worker level. Even though Gary was sincere, Williams counseled, his message was not being communicated by his submanagers to the worker level. Williams said he had been "inside" U.S. Steel and felt that the workers listened to the union organizers as a "defensive measure" against unjust treatment by management. With "leaders" rather than "drivers" for foremen, and with a shorter workday and more effective communications with workers, Williams felt that labor-management relations would improve.[9] Unfortunately, what Williams prescribed required fertile soil and a period of nurturance before industrial peace could be brought forth. In the case of the steel industry in 1919, this advice came too late to avoid a strike.

Like previous steel strikes, the one in 1919 was a violent confrontation that did nothing to improve the future. Gary maintained that the issue was the "open shop," the right of workers not to join, as well as to join, the union.[10] Gary and others in the steel industry charged that William Z. Foster, a leader of the strike committee, was an anarchist who sought the overthrow of the American economic system. Within the labor movement, Samuel Gompers played his role in a minor key so that the AFL would not be connected too closely with Foster.[11] When Foster, the most active of the strike's leaders, was discredited by his anarchist activities, public support for the strike dissipated. Within a month, the steel mills were operating at 75 to 90 percent of capacity as some workers returned. By January 1920, the steel strike was broken but continued ill will would lead to other attempts in a climate more favorable to strikes.

While Williams had a sound grasp of the causes of discontent, the grudges had persisted for too long to lend themselves to a quick solution. The solutions that Williams advocated required a period of time and a measure of trust between labor and management in order to become effective. The lesson for Williams in the steel strike of 1919 was that his ideas and experiences needed exposure to a broader audience before they could be used to forestall future crises.

Comparing Industrial Societies

Whiting Williams loved to travel, and his year in Berlin and his association with the Oberlin College Travel Bureau had given him experience in the cultures and languages of Europe. The reports by the "hobo" had been well received by government officials, industrialists, labor leaders, and the public. Why not, thought Williams, see if the hobo could investigate labor in other countries to determine if the American scene was unique or if there were similarities across international boundaries? In this type of thinking, Williams was far ahead of others in the emerging field of human and industrial relations.

Travel abroad in the disguise of a laborer posed problems, however, for Great Britain and the European countries insisted upon their workers having work permits, identity cards, passports, or other such paraphernalia of identity verification. To overcome this handicap, Williams asked prominent U.S. businesspeople and government officials for letters of introduction to their counterparts or acquaintances abroad. Armed with these, Williams made contacts and asked them to introduce him to the owners and managers of the places he wanted to work. The owners and managers then knew why Williams was there, thus overcoming the work permit problem, but the workers were not to be made aware of Williams's true identity. How to fool the workers? Here, Williams's knowledge of French, German, and Spanish was of help, but not of enough help to keep him from being pegged as an outsider. In France, Williams overcame this problem in a very interesting way: if a worker asked him why he was working there, he would respond *"J'ai une amie"* ("I have a lady friend"), and the French workers would wink knowingly, smile, and nudge each other as if this explained everything. In Great Britain and Germany, Williams did not use this ploy, and he did have some problems. He was, however, making his first foray into the study of comparative industrial relations.

Full Up and Fed Up

Williams's experience with working twelve-hour shifts in the American steel industry had made him a fervent proponent of the movement for an eight-hour workday. The iron and steel industry in Great Britain was now on an eight-hour shift system, so why not see how it was working? Similarly, Williams could check the pulse of unrest in British industry and compare it to his experiences of the previous year in America. As introductions, Williams had letters from John P. Frey, editor of the *Iron Molder's Journal*, and Harlow S. Person, managing director of the Taylor Society. Frey remarked that Williams had "a firm grasp on the problems of workers," and that he merited assistance in his study of the British iron industry.[12]

Williams spent three months (from June 29 through September 24, 1920) living his double life at the coal mines of South Wales, the docks of Glasgow, Scotland, and the steel mills of Middlesborough, Newcastle, and Sheffield, England. He found that strikes were more numerous in Great Britain and that radicalism in the labor movement was more abundant. He summarized his impressions in the title of the book he wrote about his experience: *Full Up and Fed Up.* "Full up" referred to his conclusion that Great Britain was a crowded nation with a shortage of decent housing and a scarcity of jobs. These conditions led to a particular outlook for labor, management, and the public which was like in some ways, but different from in more ways, the outlook he found in the United States. "Fed up" referred to Williams's impression that certain factors in education, class distinctions, fatigue, and labor-management relations led people to become disgusted with the situation in which they found themselves and to resort to certain types of responses that did not always result in peaceful solutions to labor problems.

Williams marveled at how crowded Great Britain was, with a population one-half the size of the U.S. population living and working in a space only twice the size of the state of Ohio. Housing was poor, especially in the boarding houses and hotels for workers, where sheets were changed every fortnight, whether they needed it or not! Personal cleanliness of the workers also bothered Williams, who reported that the miners considered it "unsafe and unhygienic" to wash their backs. One miner told Williams, "Well, I *know* w'at 'appens [when he washed his back]. With me 'tis no argument. Both 'ave I tried, washin' and no washin', and I *know* that washin' do give me a cold!"[13]

In addition to uncleanliness and overcrowding, Williams found that the workers in Great Britain perceived job scarcity to a greater extent than did their counterparts in America. "In the days of war," one unemployed worker on the Glasgow docks explained,

> it was fine here, because men were scarce and jobs were plentiful,
> with high wages. Now since the war, of course, there are plenty
> of jobs, but there are plenty of men too. [What] this docker

business means is that you must come down every morning, and
you must go to the dock and wait and see if there is any chance.
It would seem to me to be the finest possible world to live in, if a
man could get out of bed in the morning and know that there was
a job waitin' for him.[14]

This scarcity of jobs also led workers to resist technological advancement in the form of laborsaving devices and to resist the introduction
of any scientific management–motivated attempts to make jobs more
efficient. Payment by results, or piecework payment, was also fought
because it was believed that these incentives led some people to work
other people out of jobs, as per the lump of labor theory. As one
worker expressed it: "Iverybody should take their turn—iverybody
should divide up and iverybody should 'ave 'is share of work."[15]

Unions were seen as one way to achieve this goal of sharing work;
another avenue was through the Labour party and the nationalization
of industry, especially in coal, steel, telephone, and transport. The
government, according to the workers, had the responsibility to create
and guarantee jobs for everyone. Such socialistic sentiments, Williams noted, emphasized security and not the desire for opportunity
that he had observed in America.

American workers also followed the lump of labor notion but
had never resisted piecework and scientific management as the
workers had in Britain. Why? American workers had formed numerous unions, but these unions had never sought to become a separate
political party, nor was there any pronounced move to nationalize
industry. Why? What factors, wondered Williams, made the American and British workers different, even though they both had the same
language (well, almost) in addition to a common cultural heritage?

The answer that Williams provided can be reduced to basically
one factor—class consciousness. Williams did, however, recognize
that this awareness had many facets. American workers, Williams
felt, had never viewed themselves as a "working class," apart from the
rest of society. Through education and hard work, a worker in
America had a "job elevator," which could bring better housing and
other manifestations of a higher standard of living. In Britain, no
such elevator existed: education was reserved for a certain class of
people and was limited for others. One miner explained to Williams
that "if I give my boy more schooling he'll not earn a farthing more as
a miner for it, and all he can become is a clerk or a teacher. And at
either of these he'll earn considerably less than as a miner. So there
you are!"[16]

Education, for those who could acquire it, was different also. One employer reflected on his education as follows:

> No, I hardly say that my education has done much for me, you know, in my present responsibilities as the manager of my father's business. Like every other boy born in my class, I spent the years between twelve and fourteen at a public school—I suppose you Americans would call it anything but a public school, because it is the sort of school attended only by the sons of the upper class—like the chaps you read about, you know, at Harrow and Eton—schools where the Iron Duke said the battle of Waterloo was won, and all that sort of thing. Well, at these public schools the studying is mostly Latin and such things—very classical and all that. . . . Of course, it does give a man a fine lot of acquaintances with the others of the same set about the country, and I dare say that's worth while. But now, of course, my job is to get on, not with that set but with our workers, isn't it?[17]

Williams concluded that the gap between labor and management was greater than he had observed in America. The lack of a job elevator was one cause of this gap and the nature of education in Great Britain was another factor. Williams felt that the British should emphasize "industrial enterprise," rather than the classics, in order to prepare people for jobs as managers. The distance between labor and management could never be decreased until the emphasis in both education and industry was on opportunity, not on security and social position. Britain had never developed business schools to prepare people for positions of managerial responsibility and to teach them the importance of understanding and dealing with the worker.

The outward signs of the distance between labor and management were strikes and low productivity. In coal mining, for example, America had 735,000 miners who mined 700 million tons of coal, while in Great Britain 1.2 million miners could produce only 230 million tons of coal. This lower productivity, combined with rising labor costs, was pricing British coal out of the world market.

Williams did admire the progress the British had made in eliminating the twelve-hour shift from the iron and steel industry. While American industry in 1920 still had twelve-hour shifts, the British steelworkers' union had made some progress as early as 1896 toward eliminating the twelve-hour shift. In 1919, national legislation had completed the abolition of "long turns" in steel. Williams found that eight-hour shifts in the British steel industry had improved employer-employee relations, reduced fatigue, created 50 percent more jobs (that is, the number of workers needed for three, eight-hour shifts was 50 percent greater than the number needed for two, twelve-hour shifts), and increased profitability. For workers who made less than fifty shillings per week (five shillings = one U.S. dollar in 1920), employers made up the difference between the eight-hour and twelve-hour shifts, so that the workers' weekly wages would not be reduced. More highly paid workers, however, did experience reduced wages as a result of reduced hours, as did those who were paid by "tonnage," a piece rate.

All in all, Williams found that the experience of the British steel industry had been positive, and he believed that America should follow the example of its British cousins.[18] He did have some doubts about how the British workers would spend their increased leisure time, since there were few places the working classes frequented other than the pubs and the racing tracks. The evils of "drink," one of those items that kept poor people poor according to the Social Gospel, was one of Williams's favorite topics. He commented that the British were heavy bettors and hard drinkers and that this kept them from using their money and time on more enlightening endeavors. One of Williams's favorite stories involved the Scotsman's answer to the question of why he drank whiskey and beer together. "Uf Ah drinks whuskee aloon [alone], then Ah'm droonk afoor Ah'm foo' [full]. Uf Ah drinks beer aloon, then Ah'm foo' afoor Ah'm droonk. Wi' shuckeee awnd beer, Ah'm joost fet [fit] — Ah'm both droonk awnd foo'!"[19]

The drinking problem was not solely the province of workers but could be found anywhere there was a dissatisfaction with life. For workers, drink was often a means to escape more unpleasant things: "The drunker ye be [one worker told Williams] the less ye'll be a-mindin' of th' flies and bugs. And when ye sober up, ye're used to 'em. See?"[20] Williams found in the British steel industry that there was less drinking on the eight-hour shift than there had been previously, since the workers needed less "relief" from the long shifts. Despite this lessening of drinking, Williams still feared that too much leisure time for the British worker would mean more time at the tracks and in the pubs.

While Williams admired the effects of the eight-hour movement in Britain, he maintained that serious problems resided in that country, especially in the relationship between management and the workers. The working class was fed up with its position in society and sought, through unions and the nationalization of industry, to improve its status. Managers, not having the benefit of an education that would prepare them to deal in an understanding fashion with their employees, saw the union and nationalization movements as threats to their established positions in society. Both groups sought to protect and to ration their share. Williams proposed something different: he observed that the focus should be on creating new products and markets in industry rather than on the government spreading the work around. He cited the automobile industry as an emerging one (remember that this was in 1920), which would lead to new jobs and new markets. Already, in Coventry, England, automobile factories were paying seven pounds, ten shillings (about thirty dollars) per week to their workers, more than they could make in the declining coal and steel industries. While the supply of natural resources helped to explain the relatively greater prosperity of America vis à vis Great Britain, Williams concluded that the greater difference was in "spiritual resources," which, in America, led to a spirit of "initiative and progress" rather than to the security orientation of the British.[21] In this insightful, comparative study of industrial societies, Williams had identified some of the causes of unrest, the different outlooks of workers, and differing causes of national prosperity.

Horny Hands and Hampered Elbows

The next field of investigation for Whiting Williams was Europe, where he used letters of introduction from such luminaries as the management consultant, H. K. Hathaway, labor leader Samuel Gompers, Ohio's Governor Harry L. Davis, and the U.S. Secretary of Commerce, Herbert Hoover.[22] Williams's tour of Europe would take him through coal mines and steel mills in France, Belgium, Germany, and the Saar (then a protectorate of the League of Nations but under French control). The results of his travels, and his comparison of European with British and American workers, provided a cross section of industrial and human relations during this period. Williams took the title for the book of his findings from the callouses (horny hands) and scrapes (hampered elbows) he received digging coal in France.[23]

After more than two months in Europe (from July 20 to September 30, 1921), Williams reported more similarities than differences among the countries of France, Belgium, and Germany. The Europeans, he felt, were more like the British than like the Americans, probably because of the recently concluded war. In many places there was evidence of the conflict — expanded cemeteries, relics of weapons and barbed wire, leveled buildings, and flooded coal mines. In all places, labor-management relations were affected more by the leftovers of war than by any other factor. In France, some 1.8 million war dead created a serious labor shortage, which retarded the nation's economic recovery. Williams did see some hope for the future of business leadership in France because its young men were changing their career aspirations from government service to "insisting upon going into business."

> That is causing trouble in the families, but it will be the families that will give way and not the youths. For it is they who have on their side all the thrust of France's future. There is a real possibility that these young men will give to the factory, office, and the banking-room exactly that touch of idealism which business [in France] so much needs. It is something of this that we Americans have put into industry and commerce to an extent unequalled by any other nation. We have found that spirit in business because we have to find it somewhere, and we have not had time to look elsewhere. The French have found it outside of business because they did not care to find anything in business except what was necessary to existence. It would be immensely helpful to the world's peace if France's "generation of the victory" could avail to combine the practical and the ideal in a new and higher species of business technic [sic].[24]

Increasing radicalism in French unions in the postwar era had led to more labor strife than Williams had observed anywhere else. The largest French union, the *Confédération Générale du Travail,* was split between the conservative socialists and the radical communists, leading to more disarray among the workers. Williams had little trouble getting jobs in France because of the labor shortage. He found the workers to be openly critical of management, as well as of the government; and they complained constantly about the high cost of living as postwar inflation swept Europe. Williams observed that it took one-half of his wages to pay for his room and board; a suit of overalls cost one and one-half day's wages; and to put half soles on a pair of shoes cost three-fourths of a day's pay. He felt that these costs were typical for most French workers and that this contributed to the industrial unrest.

France also fell short, in Williams's opinion, in its "amenities," such as telephones, indoor plumbing, and the means of disposing of garbage. He also took notice (and it was rare for him to report observations concerning the marital or sexual behavior of the workers) of the French practice of *mariage á quatre.* In France, marriages were arranged for social position, financial security, or for both — but never for love, according to Williams. The result was the practice of *mariage á quatre*, which left the husband and wife free, provided a certain amount of discretion was exercised, to find love outside of marriage. Williams attributed the French "art of philandering" to economic scarcity, which raised parental concern for their children's financial security and social position above other needs.[25] Overall, Williams concluded that the French were hard workers who were overly concerned with security; furthermore, they needed to stop drinking so much and to improve their sanitation and plumbing facilities.

The Germans were in a vengeful mood and waiting for *der Tag*, the day of revenge against the French, the English, and all others who had imposed upon them the onerous reparations. Williams was unable to get a job in Germany, despite his letters of introduction, because the employers insisted that the workers still harbored strong anti-American sentiments. The Germans were recovering quickly (perhaps because most of the war had been fought on French soil), although the rate of inflation had been 1000 percent since the war.

Williams concluded that European workers were paid less than American workers and enjoyed fewer amenities. American workers drove to work, Europeans rode bicycles; American workers owned their own homes, the Europeans rented; 1 in 8 Americans had a telephone, but only 1 in 143 Europeans had one. Americans enjoyed the job elevator of education, but this was rare in Europe; the American worker was closer to the mainstream of the community, while the European worker was considered a class apart. In terms of labor-management relations, there was a greater social distance and a greater stress placed upon the hierarchy of authority in Europe than in America.

Why were the Europeans so different? In the main, Williams found here the same causes as in Great Britain: class consciousness, educational barriers, an emphasis on security rather than opportunity, resistance to known techniques that would improve productivity, and, finally, the relatively crowded conditions: "Europe is a crowded room — so crowded that if one nation puts its fork in its mouth it is likely to put its elbow in another nation's eye."[26] So the struggle for space continued; a decade later the plea would be for *lebensraum*, always at the point of the bayonet. Perhaps, "hampered elbows" was a double entendre and referred to the crowded continent that struggled for living space just as Williams had struggled for elbow room in a coal mine 800 feet below the earth in a vein 4 feet high.

When he decided to leave France in the autumn of 1921, Williams made arrangements to try the new air service from Paris to London. The plane had two engines, flew at 1000 feet, and took three hours to make the trip. Williams had never been in a plane before, so he admired the view. When the plane reached England, clouds obscured the airport so the pilot landed the plane in the nearest open pasture he could find. After that, Williams vowed to stick to trains!

The white collar hobo extended his investigations by comparing the American worker's mind to that of the workers in Great Britain and Western Europe. The course of the labor movement and of labor-management relations in America, compared with Great Britain and Europe, has remained remarkably consistent with what Whiting Williams found over sixty years ago. America still remains a more open society of greater opportunity for individuals to use education to cross the turbulent waters of any class, racial, religious, or other artifical distinction among humans. The American labor movement has avoided radicalization and has sought its goals through the existing political party system. Although workers (and others) have become more security conscious, America is still seen as the land of opportunity. No working class has emerged, and the distance between labor and management is still slight. It is amazing that Williams perceived these differences and their causes so accurately over sixty years ago and held forth the prospect that through greater human understanding we could improve our labor-management relations in all countries.

labor, agreed that there was no need for unemployment insurance, because "when the government undertakes the payment of money to those who are unemployed, it places in the power of the government the lives and the work and the freedom of the workers."[4] The American Federation of Labor (AFL) did support the notion of public works spending to stimulate employment. Williams, however, opposed this on the grounds that it transferred, but did not solve, the problem because the government would be taking money from taxpayers and savers, thus reducing their spending power to increase that of others.

Unemployment, Williams explained, was largely a natural phenomenon and relatively little could be done about it. There were two types of unemployment: seasonal, which was the result of forces of nature and affected agricultural and construction work especially; and cyclical, which was related to the ups and downs in the level of business activity. Since the forces of nature could not be controlled, and since the business cycle resulted largely from natural ebbs and flows in supply and demand for products, only a few things could be done: (1) train workers so that they had more skills to transfer from job to job if necessary; (2) promote thrift to provide workers with savings as a cushion against future uncertainty; and (3) "level out" industrial production to avoid the peaks and valleys of production and consumption.[5]

The general outcome of the unemployment conference was the feeling that unemployment was a state and city issue, not a federal one. Hoover did establish a Federal Bureau of Unemployment, which coordinated and encouraged the activities of governors, mayors, and directors of federal government agencies who could find jobs for people.[6] The immediate effect was not dramatic, but a decline in the level of unemployment did become apparent. The official figure (an annual average) for 1922 was 2,859,000 unemployed, some 6.7 percent of the total labor force. After 1922, however, unemployment never again rose above 5 percent until 1930.

In brief, Williams recognized that unemployment was a multifaceted problem that affected people in economic, social, and spiritual ways. This "spiritual" interpretation closely resembles what we refer to today as the "mental health" aspects of unemployment. America remains primarily a work-oriented culture that values those who work and denigrates those who do not. Thus, the social system puts pressure on the unemployed, and a person's internal guidance system suggests that work is better than idleness. From his experiences and from those of others, Williams knew the importance of work to one's physical and mental well-being.

The Railroad Strike of 1922: Working Both Sides

As the unemployment problems of 1921 faded, wages became a greater issue and led to two major national strikes in 1922. In April, the United Mine Workers Union led some 500,000 coal miners off the job in a dispute over wage reductions. Employment in the industry had declined in the face of newly developing power sources such as petroleum and natural gas, and the union sought to maintain wages despite less market demand for coal. While the coal miners were on strike, trouble brewed in the railroad industry. During World War I, the federal government had taken over the operation of the railroads and had established means of settling disputes between labor and management. Under federal administration, nationwide standardized agreements concerning wages, hours, and working conditions were established. Furthermore, barriers to union membership were removed, and the AFL was able to reap a bonanza of members for its Railway Employees Department.

After the war, the Transportation Act of 1920 (the Esch-Cummins Act) returned the ownership and operation of the railroads to private industry. The Railroad Labor Board, with members from labor, management, and the public, was established to mediate disputes. In 1920, the board granted large wage increases to labor to resolve a deadlock; in 1921 and 1922, however, the board mandated wage reductions at the request of management, which was beset by declining economic conditions. The irony of the ensuing dispute was that it was the government, rather than the railroads, that should have been blamed for the strike. During the war, when the railroads had been owned and operated by the government, wages for railroad workers had been frozen. The government did not wish to increase wages for fear of having to raise freight rates, which President Wilson felt he did not have the authority to do. As a consequence, railroad workers' wages lagged behind wages in other industries — for example, a machinist in industry received a minimum of eighty cents per hour, but in a railroad shop, the minimum was only sixty-eight cents per hour in 1919.[7]

The Railway Employees Department of the AFL represented most of the employees whose wages were cut in 1921 and 1922. On

July 1, 1922, a strike of some 400,000 nonoperating railroad workers began, the first nationwide rail strike since 1894.[8] Although the non-operating employee unions were on strike, the operating brother-hoods refused to join the strike, lending an air of confusion to the dispute.[9] A total of nearly one million workers from the coal and railroad industries were on strike, yet the trains were still running. Some farsighted railroad managers recognized, however, that this type of conflict and confusion had to be remedied by some means involving both short- and long-run solutions.

WORKING FOR THE BALTIMORE AND OHIO. Daniel Willard, president of the Baltimore and Ohio (B&O) Railroad, was one of those progressive managers who sought to reduce labor-management conflict. He had come to his position "through the ranks": his first job was on a track gang and he rose to fireman and later to engineer before he moved into positions involving managerial responsibility.[10] Having been a worker enabled Willard to relate to the workers' needs, to be sympathetic to their grievances, and to establish improved rela-tions between labor and management. These experiences as a worker also attracted him to employing Whiting Williams to study the strik-ing workers and find out what was on their minds.

It was agreed that Williams would get his job without any inter-vention by Willard in order to protect his anonymity: "Helped by my seediest clothes and proper carelessness with collar and razor, I got hired surprisingly easily—aided by my working pedigree as an unfor-tunate worker laid off from a certain factory job by the coal short-age."[11] His job paid forty-four cents per hour and he became a store-room helper in a B&O freight station where his duties involved

> the rating of clerk, but the Amalgamated Order of Draymen and Coal Heavers—or whatever it may be—certainly had good grounds for a jurisdictional dispute—I did one or maybe two of them out of a job. After eight hours juggling kegs of nails, car-boys of sulphuric acid, or barrels and boxes of crowbars and tools around with a truck, it was a delight to spend the ninth hour "reddin' up the place" with a broom and a sprinkling can. For the past week I've had little skin left on my knees, from lifting—with my buddy—212-pound kegs of spikes up into their place on the third level.[12]

From the performance of such jobs, Williams was able to apply his shirt sleeve empiricism and learn more about how the workers felt. He reported that the workers were in full support of the B&O. The "eastern railroads" were the cause of the problem, according to the workers, because of poorer labor-management relations. Morale was good and Williams reported that most of the B&O employees he encountered felt that the strike was unnecessary and the result of a minority sentiment among the union members. "We fellows don't like to strike," said a brakeman.

> You can see for yourself we aren't roughnecks. But it just don't seem possible to get the public to think about us fellows in any other way. We've got to make them [the public] uncomfortable. When we tie the country up and make it stand still a couple of days, then they begin to wake up and ask what's the matter?[13]

Williams reported that a primary concern among the B&O workers was seniority. He quoted a fireman to illustrate the importance of this facet of employment:

> Why, without that [seniority], why should anybody work for a livin' on a railroad? That and the choice of a job your time gives you—that's all that makes it a job. Here's me on a good run gettin' my $200 a month—that's because of my twelve years, see?—and then you come along, that never fired a mile, and takes it from me. That's be nice, now, wouldn't it? Huh, I should say not![14]

Williams reported to Willard that the employees would like some assurance about what would happen to the seniority system since strikebreakers had been hired to fill some positions. If the workers on strike returned, how would the seniority system be affected?[15] This sort of intelligence gathering by Williams later enabled Willard to bring about a rapprochement between labor and management in the railway strike of 1922.

Williams spent two months as a B&O worker. He assessed the company's public relations, as well as its relations with labor. The company enjoyed continued customer goodwill despite the strike, and Williams predicted that the B&O's competitive situation would improve after the strike because of the sound relations and cooperation that existed between labor and management.[16] Indeed, the B&O ultimately did emerge from the strike in a much better condition than it had entered it. But labor would also need the help of the white collar hobo before the strike ended.

GETTING LABOR'S POINT OF VIEW. Although a federal injunction declared the strike illegal and the strikers to be without jobs, the strike continued. Williams was approached at that point by *Collier's* magazine and asked to do a series of "inside" stories, but for both sides; that is, to investigate both those on strike and those who were working to break the strike. Since Williams had good relations with organized labor, he was fearful of becoming a strikebreaker, so he asked his friend, AFL president Samuel Gompers, for advice. Gompers urged Williams to investigate both sides and provided a letter for Williams to use in case of an emergency.[17]

After donning once again his "seediest clothes," Williams responded to an advertisement that promised free room and board, a bonus of up to two dollars a day, and generous overtime for anyone who would come to work for the railroad to replace the strikers. As Williams crossed the union picket line in the guise of a worker coming to work he received his worst scare. A picketing union member threatened:

> Buddy, has anyone taken the trouble to tell you that you have taken your life in your hands in coming to work in this place? Has anybody given you the low-down on the dynamite that goes off in here where you are supposed to earn your daily bread? — that is, as long as you last. Of course, you understand that we guys on the outside haven't the faintest idea exactly how many goddam scabs [strikebreakers] get killed when it goes off, because the goddam company buries all the corpses at night and we can't count the exact number.[18]

Despite the threat, Williams and other strikebreakers crossed the picket line under police escort. Williams was assigned the job of "car knocker," which meant that he used a wrench to knock on wheels, bolts, couplings, etc., to see if anything was loose, and if so, he fixed it. He and his fellow strikebreakers, "scabs" to those who were on strike, lived in a bunkhouse, up to one hundred of them in one large room. Guards patrolled the living and work areas and there was a high wooden fence to keep the picketers away from the strikebreakers. In one incident, the picketers set fire to the fence in an effort to reach the strikebreakers and to do them bodily harm. A fortuitous rain put the fire out, however, before any damage could be done. Williams noted that being a strikebreaker had its "anxious moments."

Williams remarked that the strikebreakers fell into four different categories: there were "finks," professional strikebreakers who were young, aggressive, ready for a fight, and who made top dollar going from strike to strike, living dangerously. A second type included "junkers," "snow birds," and "dope fiends" — people who worked long enough to buy their "fix" and then left. Another group consisted of immigrants, recently arrived, who took the job because they could not find another. The fourth group was a surprising one—sober, responsible, and hardworking, these were men who were either actually on strike or out of work and needed the job, so they changed their names and made a temporary relocation in order to become strikebreakers. One worker, who had been on strike in his home community, explained his situation:

> Four weeks I stayed out with the boys—believin' the leaders that every day they were goin' to win. If I'd 'a' been single, I'd 'a' stuck till the cows come home. Without a wife, a fellow can beg, borrow, steal, or bum and still stand by his mates. But what is a fellow goin' to do when his wife and two kids—after four weeks, you understand?—begin to say: "Daddy, I just got to have a pair of shoes," or, "Papa, how shall I start to school without a new dress?" A fellow's just got to do something then, I tell you; he's just got to.[19]

Yet another was out of work:

> Carpenterin' is my [normal] line, but slack work in my town made me think right smart of this easy money. If you don't take it too easy, they may make you a foreman, like they did me. Last night my two helpers hid themselves after midnight and slept till mornin'. I'll do my best to give you overtime. Sometimes I've worked a plumb twenty-four hours—and got paid for thirty-two. That's $22.40. At that rate I'll clean up around $500 in six weeks—and no place to spend it so long as we're gettin' free board and room at the camp—and takin' no chances on gettin' a cracked nut by tryin' to get uptown past these here pickets outside.[20]

Another of those strikebreaking workers explained the complexities of job and community in this way: "If we turn down the boss and stick by our buddies, we may have to get another job. But if we stick by the boss and turn down our buddies—why, then, we're just yellow. We gotta leave town, gotta sell our house and everything, and start all over again somewhere else."[21] So it was easier to appear to be on strike in their home community and thereby save face with their fellow workers. The necessities of working, however, meant that they would go elsewhere, change their name, and become a strikebreaker. Once the crisis had passed, they could return to their former community.

After gathering information from the strikebreaker's point of view, Williams changed his location to Parkersburg, West Virginia, in order to walk the picket line with the strikers. Their viewpoints, as might be expected, were that the wage cuts were unfair, that the government had no right to issue an injunction against the strike, and that management's employment of strikebreakers was a threat to the security of the union members. Another issue, related to the questions of seniority and security, was that of work jurisdictions. Traditionally, craft unions had made arrangements with other craft unions to determine to whom certain jobs belonged. In some cases, this became a matter of the negotiated contract with management, although in most cases it was a matter of customary practice. From management's point of view, these jurisdictions were stultifying and expensive:

> How can we ever fix engines at decent cost [a railway executive asked], when for some little defect we may have to call in a sheet-metal worker to remove the sheathing and the lagging or asbestos stuffing from the outside of the boiler, then a pipe fitter to unscrew a pipe, then a machinist to fix a little valve, and then perhaps a boiler maker to tighten a stay bolt?[22]

The strikers took the position that these rules about work jurisdictions were formulated to protect the workers' rights to their jobs by preventing encroachment by others. The argument of the craft workers resembled very closely Whiting Williams's earlier conclusions about the job consciousness of unions. One of the craft workers explained that

> the rules—the craft rules signed up with the railways—allow for all that [i.e., craft jurisdictions]. The reason is that if they don't, some hard-boiled master mechanic takes advantage and starts us eating the heart out of each other's jobs. But all the boys will tell you this—and don't fail to get it—when we have a fair and square boss, then we show him we're willin' to go along with him and not bother about rules. See? Them rules is made for jams— what we all ought to do is to stop the jams before they start.[23]

While seniority had been identified as the major issue of the strike, other facets of job security, such as jurisdictions, lingered below the surface. Williams learned that the strikers developed defensive measures to offset management's activities and that sometimes some of these led to violence. One defensive measure for the strikers was an informal information network about company spies and scabs:

> We boys know the company has spies sitting in our meetings—we

soon get to spot 'em — and use 'em to ball up the enemy [a strike leader explained]. But we ain't so slow, either. We have our boys workin' all over the country in roundhouses and shops, bringin' us information about how good or bad the work is on the engines, etc. Naturally, it cheers the bunch up good. A lot of clerks are spottin' some of our strikers who are strike breaking at other points. Just lately we located one out in Nevada. Word about him comes to Chicago because, y'see, he's too good a worker not to be a regular shopman. We'd already sent to Chicago for information about a chap here that's missin'. We send his photograph out to Nevada and, sure 'nough, it's him. Yes, he'll probably have a few bad days before he gets back.[24]

Violence, though contrary to official union policy, was one way of dealing with strikebreakers. "The minute our mine signed up," one of the striking miners said,

a gang went out and beat up a dozen or so that's been scabbin'. You'd oughta saw it. One of 'em went fourteen feet before he come down! All last week we been takin' our guns and goin' up where some scabs was workin' outside — possum huntin'. No shootin', but still, the rest of 'em in mines that ain't signed up better get t'ell outa here, I'll say.[25]

While Williams walked the picket line, an agreement was finally reached in the coal dispute. This brought some relief to the nation, but the railroad unions continued to strike in defiance of the government. Someone who could mediate a solution was needed: that role was assumed by Daniel Willard, president of the Baltimore and Ohio Railroad. In cooperation with Bert M. Jewell, president of the Railway Employees Department of the AFL, an agreement was reached whereby railway employees would be restored to their jobs "whole," that is, with their seniority and wages as they existed before the strike.[26] The "Willard-Jewell formula" for railway peace bore a remarkable resemblance to what Whiting Williams had told Willard earlier — that the workers were more concerned with seniority and job status than anything else. The Willard-Jewell formula was not an overnight success, but by November some 100 railroads had signed the agreement and some 225,000 strikers had been restored "whole." In essence, the end of the strike was a rollback, a return to previous circumstances, and it was largely a defeat for the Railway Employees Department of the AFL. Some companies, most notably the Pennsylvania Railroad, formed company unions, thus ousting the AFL. From the results, however, it was obvious that some other avenues should be provided to promote industrial peace.

Cooperation and Representation in Industry

It would be unrealistic to expect that in a free society peace will always prevail, especially between management and labor. Rather, the task of such a society is to develop means to resolve conflict in a manner befitting the notions of human choice and individual dignity. In labor-management relations this would mean that workers not be coerced into jobs, that their self-respect be supported, and that they be paid not less than their marginal product; neither should management be constrained in the exercise of its best judgment with respect to the allocation of resources necessary to attain organizational objectives. Indeed, under these circumstances, labor and management have similar goals, each needing the other. Without industry, labor is without jobs; without labor, industry is without its most vital resource.

Recognition of this mutuality of interests is not always apparent to the respective parties, and conflict is often the result. How the parties can be brought to recognize their mutual interests is a matter of both historical and contemporary interest. To serve those interests, it is helpful to examine some ideas that were evolving at the time, as well as the role that Whiting Williams played.

In 1900, the National Civic Federation (NCF) had been formed to promote more harmonious relations between labor and management. The NCF sought to mediate disputes, educate the public about labor-management relations, improve industrial relations, and demonstrate the mutual interests of labor and management. The NCF was successful in its early efforts, but by 1916 it had been pushed into a less influential role.[27] After the war it would be replaced largely by two developments: union-management cooperation and employee representation through shop councils.

Union-management cooperation was the product of a number of postwar developments: the unsuccessful strikes of 1919, which had aimed to expand union membership; a sharp economic downturn and widespread unemployment in 1921; and the unsuccessful railroad strike of 1922. Under the Willard-Jewell formula, peace was restored to most, but not all, of the nation's railroads. The leaders of organized labor saw that the momentum gained during the prounion government of the Wilson years was now gone. The response of organized labor was to cooperate with management with the proviso that the workers could elect representatives and bargain collectively. Management could install more efficient methods to improve productivity provided that labor would be recognized and involved. This was a defensive strategy for the unions in the sense that it would help reduce their membership losses, and it offered possibilities of organizing the unorganized once a more favorable climate for unionization had appeared.[28]

Successful union-management cooperation could be found in the clothing trades and in the railroads.[29] The B&O Plan, as the Willard-Jewell formula came to be known, represented the best thinking in union-management cooperation. The plan spread to the Canadian National Railways, the Chicago and North Western Railroad, and the Chicago, Milwaukee, and St. Paul line, all with remarkable success.[30] Williams had assisted Willard by indicating the importance of seniority, a key feature of the settlement formula, and Williams had supported the notion that union leaders were responsible representatives of the worker. He reminded his readers that workers join unions for job security and protection against unreasonable employers. Most labor leaders were "honest, responsible, and patriotic," not bomb-waving anarchists. Both labor and management needed to come to an understanding of each other.[31]

The best example of mutual understanding, in Williams's opinion, was on the B&O Railroad. Williams continued to advise Willard on employee relations and morale. He developed plans for recognizing employees and building company pride through an internal news magazine for B&O employees that would keep workers abreast of company plans and provide a column for President Willard to state company "ideals." The *B&O Neighbor*, as he proposed, would also provide a medium for employees to be recognized. A contest should be held for the adoption of a company song and a central department should be established to handle grievances.[32] Williams praised the B&O for its success in achieving peace through cooperation. By getting the workers involved in making suggestions that could improve productivity, Williams reported that costs were down and wages were up and that the workers shared in the company's prosperity. Labor-management cooperation was the frontier of a new era of human relations.[33]

While union-management cooperation plans involved organized labor, the idea of employee representation and participation through shop councils and committees emerged as another approach for achieving industrial cooperation. The roots of the employee representation movement were in part a continuation of the paternalism of the "industrial betterment" movement, in part a hope for restoration of the prewar "open shop" days when unions had little influence, and in part a renewal of the old Social Gospel theme that labor and management could coexist peacefully if they recognized their common purpose and obeyed the golden rule. In the waning days of his term of office, President Woodrow Wilson had appointed two industrial commissions to investigate the conflict-laden year of 1919.[34] The second conference, vice-chaired by Herbert Hoover, concluded with an endorsement by employers of the idea of workers being represented through employee-elected shop councils. These councils would give workers a voice, through their chosen representatives, in matters at work that concerned their welfare. Shop councils would also give workers a choice to be represented without having to join a union and pay dues. Hoover disagreed with the unionists who felt that shop councils were antiunion. Hoover felt that shop councils provided an alternative for workers who wished a voice and a choice in the economic system.[35]

Hoover wrote to Williams that he had read *What's On the Worker's Mind?* "from end to end [and it] illuminated many dark corners and has made a great impression on me." Williams's ideas formed a good argument in support of shop councils, which would "create a switch by which people could gain a hearing over the inhuman foreman and a right of direct representation." Hoover felt that shop councils would air the grievances that Williams reported had been stifled.[36]

Worker participation and representation through shop councils was a manifestation of an abiding concern by many employers that employees needed a stake in the action. Williams had expressed earlier the shock he would feel if a supervisor ever asked him what he thought about a problem at work. Williams had observed that foremen typically assumed that workers were not paid "to think," and so the ideas of those closest to the work were never solicited. In the supervisor's mind was a fear of losing authority if workers were consulted about work, since supervisors were supposed to know everything.[37] Union leaders also resisted shop councils, but for a different reason—fear that if workers had a voice in matters affecting their welfare they would no longer see the need to pay dues to a union to represent their interests.[38]

The Russell Sage Foundation sponsored numerous studies of employee representation plans, and these studies typically reported lower worker turnover, a shared prosperity between employee and employer, better channels for handling grievances, and a voice for workers.

Some dangers were noted, such as employers with unrepentant anti-union tendencies who tried to dominate the shop councils.[39] Still, by 1924 there were some 814 employee representation plans in existence, covering some 1.5 million workers.[40] Despite opposition by union leaders, who felt employee representation plans were a "delusion and a snare," these plans prepared the way for the idea that workers could be productively involved in their companies.[41] The notion of shop councils would lead Williams to his involvement in work simplification programs. While Williams favored union-management cooperation and employee representation as avenues to recognizing the mutual interests of worker and manager, he also cautioned against mistaking these schemes as panaceas or as substitutes for his Eleventh Commandment. Regardless of the avenue chosen (that is, whether it was union-management cooperation or shop councils), Williams warned that neither could replace the need for personal contacts between the workers and their first-line supervisors:

> Be careful you don't play into the hands of the unions by trying to keep your relations with groups of workers entirely on the old individualistic basis, denying them the right of some kind of collective or representative dealing through shop committees or otherwise.

> Don't let *any* form of representative dealing, whether with shop committees or unions, cause you to forget for one moment the prime importance of maintaining close personal and individual contacts and relationships between your workers and the company as personified to the employees by your carefully chosen and continuously trained foremen. Continue to build these representatives of the company so that through them the workers will know what the company itself looks like—and so that they will like its looks.

> Consider every individual grievance that comes to the committees as a proof of a failure of those representatives of you and the company—that is, of every foreman and other officer to perform properly his true function as contact-point interpreters. In other words, have the committees or the union as a guarantee of your good faith, but try to make them, so far as possible, unnecessary to the happiness and self-respect and efficiency of the men. If you can't do this, don't blame the leaders too much for building up the collective plan into a wall between yourselves and your individual constituents.[42]

Neither shop councils nor union-management cooperation plans could replace the need for the proper relationship between management and the worker. These devices could keep the relationship from getting worse, but they alone could not make it better.

John Barleycorn

The Social Gospel, as socially conscious Protestantism, indicated that the greatest evil facing workers was "drink," the consumption of alcoholic beverages or, as they were known at the time, "John Barleycorn." As Richard T. Ely, one of the early proponents of the Social Gospel, put it: "Drink [is] the poor man's curse so often, and so often the rich man's shame."[43] Progressivism, the successor to the Social Gospel in twentieth-century America, established Prohibition as a part of its platform because alcohol undermined moral behavior, detracted from religious character development, contributed to crime and disease, and kept the poor poor.[44] The culmination of this drive to ban the distillation, sale, and consumption of alcoholic beverages was the Eighteenth Amendment to the Constitution of the United States, which received its required number of state ratifications in January 1919.

Williams, who had imbibed the Social Gospel at Oberlin College, was a teetotaler until he was in his sixties.[45] Since America was ostensibly "dry," Williams's first chance to observe the workers and John Barleycorn in action was during his visit to Great Britain in 1921. In a poor section of Glasgow, Williams observed that

> after the saloons were closed at nine the majority of the adult population appeared drunk. A walk down the street was a slow and crowded progress from one brawl or near-brawl to another. One man leaned out of a tenement window and whistled for the police because his wife had stabbed him. When the bobby came he waited for another before going up—he had had experience. Saddest of all it was to see the young girls apparently having a pleasant evening laughing at one fallen drunken man or one vanquished fighter after another—unless it was sadder to see the bareheaded and barefooted children, with the bent in or bent out little legs of rickets, the "poverty disease," getting into the midst of every crowd or else toddling along whimpering on the hand of a mother, herself drunk, while carrying a baby sleeping on her bosom.[46]

Williams found the heaviest drinking among those workers who held the dirtiest, hottest, and most repugnant jobs.[47] His conclusion, which may sound naive today, was that the harder the work, the harder the drinking needed to escape its unpleasantness. Thus, alcoholism was "the working man's curse." He thought that "we needn't bother so much about the white-collared workers. Their thirst is more or less phony."[48] To reduce alcoholism, according to Williams, legal means would be only partially successful unless accompanied by elimination of the most unpleasant aspects of jobs in industry, such as twelve-hour shifts. The benefits to the worker of abstaining were many, according to Williams: less absenteeism, greater savings of money, more time for reading and self-education, and fewer industrial accidents. In short, "The Prohibition Amendment is giving the country's less fortunate man, woman, and child a better chance than ever before to be a better, abler, more efficient, better dressed, better educated citizen."[49] Organized labor was generally in favor of Prohibition. Michael Tighe, president of the Amalgamated Association of Iron, Steel, and Tin Workers of America, and William Green, secretary-treasurer of the United Mine Workers, agreed with Williams that Prohibition was a good idea and that workers drank because of poor working conditions. Green added that he had observed a "very great economic and social improvement among the working people" since Prohibition.[50] The AFL did not favor repeal of Prohibition but did resolve that "light wines and beer" should be permitted — undoubtedly a position taken to sooth the unemployed in the AFL's Brewery Workers Union.[51]

American business corporations and trade associations provided considerable support for Prohibition.[52] The National Safety Council, formed in 1912 largely by the efforts of the U.S. Steel Corporation, pushed hard for Prohibition in the belief that it would increase on-the-job safety. Alcoholism was a problem for managers then, as it is now, and an abstemious work force could be expected to have fewer absences, less tardiness, and higher productivy, as well as greater safety. Prohibition had the support of organized labor, business, the government and everyone else except those who continued to consume alcoholic beverages. Later, when it appeared that the Twenty-First Amendment to the Constitution might repeal Prohibition, the American Business Men's Prohibition Foundation of Chicago began negotiations with Williams, whose task was to sound out public sentiments.[53] Before an agreement could be reached with Williams, however, the group concluded that it was too late. When Prohibition was finally repealed in 1933, Williams was regretful, for he felt that the workers would endure the depression better if they did not squander their money on liquor. Even at fifteen cents for a pint of "mooney" (moonshine, or illicit whiskey), the worker had to make a financial sacrifice.[54]

In summary, Whiting Williams provided us with a range of social, economic, and psychological commentary on life in the 1920s. After fighting "the war to end all wars," Americans would have preferred peace and stability rather than more conflict. It was a period when the federal government restored some of the emphasis on individualism following the progressivism of President Wilson. Thus Williams, and others, preferred to rely upon state and local initiatives to solve the 1921 recession — and it worked. Labor-management conflict was resolved, not by government intervention, but by the Willard-Jewell formula of union-management cooperation and by employee representation and participation through shop councils. Williams contributed to these developments. He felt that people could work out their own problems, except perhaps when it came to liquor. Workers and managers could work together productively and peacefully if they recognized their mutual interests.

In search of work as "Charlie Heitman" in 1919. (From *What's on the Worker's Mind: By One Who Put on Overalls to Find Out,* Charles Scribner's Sons, 1920)

As an American steelworker in 1919. (From *What's on the Worker's Mind: By One Who Put on Overalls to Find Out,* Charles Scribner's Sons, 1920)

Before leaving for Europe (*left*); as a coal miner near Lens,
France (*center*); and as a steelworker in France, 1921 (*right*).
(From *Horny Hands and Hampered Elbows: The Worker's
Mind in Western Europe,* Charles Scribner's Sons, 1922)

As a white collar executive (*left*) and in search of work in
Great Britain, 1920 (*right*). (From *Full Up and Fed Up: The
Worker's Mind in Crowded Britain,* Charles Scribner's Sons,
1921)

As a strikebreaker in the railway shop crafts strike of 1922.
(From the Western Reserve Historical Society, by permission)

As a member of the unemployed in 1931. (From the Western
Reserve Historical Society, by permission)

Counsel to Industry

THE 1920s were busy, productive years for Whiting Williams. He launched a new career as a consultant to industry on labor-management relations; wrote prolifically on work, workers, and the labor issues of the time; traveled to investigate the worker's mind in other countries; and still found time to lecture to various groups and at three of America's leading graduate schools of business. When Daniel Willard, president of the Baltimore and Ohio (B&O) Railroad, asked Williams to "go underground" to survey what the workers had on their minds during the railroad strike of 1922, Williams realized that other organizations might be interested in his investigative skills and knowledge of work and workers. From his writings and lectures he began to build an impressive list of clients (see Table 5.1). He opened an office at 3030 Euclid Avenue in Cleveland and hung out his shingle advertising "Counsel in Employee and Customer Relations."

The Consulting Service

The bulk of Williams's studies for his clients involved a general survey of physical working conditions and assessments of employee morale, relations between supervisors and employees, safety, internal and external communications, and employee benefit programs, as well as some general appraisal of the state of labor-management relations. His "old shirt and pants" came in handy as he ranged widely about the plant and offices, talking with as many people as possible. He almost always reported to top management, either to the president or a vice-president, and his reports pulled few punches. For example, he reported to Daniel Willard that railroad employees were especially profane and that this gave the company a bad community image.[1]

TABLE 5.1.   Clients of Williams's Consulting Service

Client	Date(s)	Type of Work
Baldwin Locomotive	1937	General survey
Baltimore and Ohio Railroad	1922, 1924, 1941	General survey
Bendix Corporation	1939	General survey
Chesapeake and Ohio Railroad	1941	Personnel selection
Cleveland Worsted Mills	1934	General survey
Commonwealth and Southern	1946	General survey
Electric Bond and Share	1927	General survey
B.F. Goodrich	1934, 1937, 1941	General survey
Graybar Electric	1926	General survey
Guaranty Trust	1926	General survey
Gulf Oil Corporation	1947	General survey
Lever Brothers	1938	General survey
Martha Textile Mills	1934	General survey
Monsanto Chemical	1937	General survey
National Coal Association	1923	Wages/Regularization of coal production
National Leather	1926	Employee morale
Northern Electric	1926	Employee morale
Ohio Bell Telephone	1941, 1943	Grievance handling
Philadelphia Electric	1933, 1939	General survey
Pittsburgh Street Railway	1927	General survey
Pullman, Inc.	1931	General survey
Republic Steel	1940	General survey
Rock Island Railroad	1924	General survey
Shell Oil	1936, 1939	Union activity and Cuban refinery
Singer Sewing Machine	1937	General survey
Standard Oil of New York	1939	Cuban refinery
Standard Oil of Ohio	1944	General survey
Swift and Company	1925	General survey
United Fruit	1923, 1924	General survey
Western Electric	1922, 1923, 1924	General survey
Youngstown Sheet and Tubing	1930	General survey

Note: This list of clients includes only those for which copies of Williams's consulting reports could be found in the Williams papers, Western Reserve Historical Society, Cleveland, Ohio, container 3, folder 4; and container 4, folders 1, 2, 3, and 4. Williams compiled two lists of clients, one included his work up to 1936 and another list was updated to 1946; these lists are in container 10, folder 6, separate from the consulting reports. In comparing these lists and the reports, no copies of reports could be found for the American Iron and Steel Institute, J. I. Case Company, Corning Glass Works, Duquesne Motors Company, General Tire and Rubber, Libbey-Owens-Ford Glass, Ohio Brass, and the Studebaker Corporation.

Some of Williams's clients asked him to come back again and again. Daniel Willard and Williams developed a relationship that lasted from 1922 until Willard's retirement in 1941. Williams followed up on the union-management cooperation program and continued to praise Willard and the B&O for their pioneering work in labor-management relations.[2] On other assignments, especially where employer-employee relations were poor, Williams would recommend either the B&O Plan or a shop council form of worker representation. For example, the Pittsburgh Street Railway Company and the Singer Sewing Machine Company received recommendations that they should move toward worker representation. He cautioned those who already had shop councils (for example, National Leather, of Boston) that these councils were not substitutes for good supervisors who cared about their workers.

Williams provided a pipeline that ran directly from the workers to top management: for example he told Standard Oil of New York that its Cuban operations were not helping ease "domestic unrest" there because Standard was paying and treating its employees poorly.[3] Another oil company client, the Shell Oil Corporation, was considered a pioneer in personnel practices in the industry. In 1918, Shell had established a Service and Employment Department to perform the personnel task, and the company was considered to have very sound labor-management relations. In 1936, however, the Oil Workers' Union of the newly formed Congress of Industrial Organizations (CIO) attempted to organize Shell's employees. Williams counseled Shell to recognize that the progress the union was making was probably a sign of the need for improved communications within the company. Williams was opposed to the CIO, for reasons which will be examined later, even though he had been a supporter of the American Federation of Labor (AFL). He maintained that unions were not bad per se, but that the CIO sought to divide labor from management rather than to seek harmonious relations. The Oil Workers' Union succeeded despite Williams's warnings, and it continued to spread its membership quite rapidly during this period. Shell placed enough credence in Williams, however, to seek his services again in 1939 with regard to its refinery in Cuba. According to Williams, Shell was paying better wages than Sinclair Oil was in Cuba, but not as well as Standard Oil, which was paying too little. He advised Shell to improve its pay and personnel practices in Cuba, just as he had advised Standard of New York.[4]

Another company, Swift, which was in an industry that was noted for its poor working conditions, also asked Williams to see if its employee relations could be improved. Swift, hoping to offset some of the adversities of its business, had been a pioneer in the "employee welfare" movement. For example, in 1912 Swift had established a guaranteed weekly wage, one of the first companies to follow this practice of trying to stabilize employment.[5] In the days following World War I, when developments had encouraged the AFL to expand its organizing efforts, an AFL affiliate, the Amalgamated Meat Cutters and Butcher Workmen of North America, tried to organize Swift and Company in addition to other packing houses. The union was opposed at Swift by an employee representation plan that would have given the worker a voice without requiring payment of union fees. A bitter strike over how the workers would be represented occurred in 1921. Strikebreakers were brought in to operate the plants. The meat cutters' union lost, declining from a membership of some 100,000 members to about 5,000 after the strike.

Against this background of poor working conditions and labor discontent Williams was brought in to advise the company. After studying operations in Kansas City, Omaha, and Chicago for five weeks, Williams suggested some ideas that he thought might help. Even though the physical working conditions probably could not be changed, a seniority system for promotions out of the slaughter pits would give workers "hope" and reduce employee turnover. More minorities, especially blacks and Italians, should be placed on the shop council to give these workers involvement in and understanding of company matters. Williams reported that the representation plan was working well, especially at the Kansas City plant, where all of the workers went to "assemblies" and "spoke up" while management listened. At "other" plants, presumably those in Omaha and Chicago, some managers refused to listen to the workers, so Williams advised that these nonlistening managers needed to hear from top management about the importance of open communications to the success of the employee representation plan. Finally, Williams recommended that the company image could be improved if it dropped such words as "offal," "slaughter," and "carcass" from all communications. Rather, the emphasis should be on "packing," the end result rather than the process.[6]

The United Fruit Company was also advised to improve its personnel policies in Costa Rica, Nicaragua, Guatemala, and Honduras. Williams said that the image of the United Fruit Company in these countries was that it was "soaking the suckers." Medical care was almost nonexistent (almost one-fourth of the employees had malaria), company housing was inadequate, and the relationship between the supervisors, all of whom were either British or American, and the local people was poor. Williams reported that the company needed to provide more worker recognition and security, better housing and medical care, more rewards for effort, and promotions of qualified local workers to supervisory positions to create social ladders for the employees.[7]

In his consulting practice, Williams had the ear of top management. Sometimes he did not have pleasant things to report, but his investigative skills were put to good use. His list of clients reads like a *Fortune 500* of its period, and this alone is witness to his esteem in the business world. From 1922 to 1947, he was active in this consulting practice; afterward, when he reached the age of seventy, he dropped that facet of his career. While but a sample of his consulting practice has been presented, his work for one company in particular, Western Electric, merits an in-depth view.

Western Electric: A Case Study

The function of the Western Electric Company, a wholly owned subsidiary of the American Telephone and Telegraph Company (AT&T), was to manufacture and supply telephones and telephone equipment for its parent company and other customers. Western Electric became famous in the 1930s for some experiments carried out at its Hawthorne plant in Cicero, a suburb of Chicago, Illinois. Most historians trace the beginnings of industrial sociology and human relations to these experiments, which identified, among other things, the importance of a human-oriented supervisory style; the importance of developing good listening skills and promoting open employee-manager communications; and the influence of recognition on employee morale and productivity. While these findings had a measurable influence on the course of management thought, the work of Whiting Williams for Western Electric from 1922 through 1924, *before* the famous Hawthorne experiments began, fills in some gaps in the historical record by showing how the company's policies and practices were already changing when the Hawthorne experiments began.

WESTERN ELECTRIC'S PERSONNEL COMMITTEE. As early as 1913, Western Electric's Hawthorne plant had an Employment and Welfare Branch that was administering the plans for employee benefits. Hawthorne had an employee restaurant, a hospital, athletic programs of every sort, a camera club, a fifty-two piece band, and other on- and off-duty programs for employees. The employee benefit fund, fully financed by the company, provided pensions, disability payments, illness payments, and benefits in the case of death. There was also an evening school at which employees could study typing, principles of electricity, accounting, English, mechanical drawing, and other practical subjects.[8] These courses were supervised by the Educational Committee of the Hawthorne Club, a group elected by the employees. In 1920, the company announced an employee savings and loan program and an employee stock-ownership plan.[9] In brief, until 1920, the company emphasized primarily the "welfare" and "industrial betterment" programs described in Chapter 1.

The year 1920, however, marked a change in Western Electric's overall personnel policy. A companywide Personnel Committee was formed, consisting of the executives who represented the main departments of the company. The chairman of the Personnel Committee was Howard A. Halligan, vice-president of the General Staff Department. The Personnel Committee was formed as a result of the rapid growth of the company, which necessitated additional personnel as well as additional plans and programs to provide for them. Its charter was to direct the conduct of personnel research and to assist in formulating and interpreting personnel policies. The committee also provided centralized, uniform guidance on personnel matters on a companywide basis.

In the spring of 1922, Western Electric employed Williams to investigate employee turnover and the wage scale at the Hawthorne plant. Williams reported that the turnover statistics, as they were being recorded at the time, were of little value: he needed data on "voluntary quits," for these data would best reflect the workers' attitudes. He also recommended the hiring of interviewers who would talk with those who had quit ("exit interviews," in today's terminology). Finally, the company needed to pay more attention to how wages of different jobs "compared to each other," for example, skilled jobs should be compared with other skilled ones, semiskilled with semiskilled, and so forth, "in order to avoid trouble" when wage changes were made.[10] On this point, Williams was recalling his experiences, which had indicated that workers were particularly sensitive to wages in a relative sense, that is, one's own wages as compared to the wages of others with similar skills. Williams explained to the Personnel Committee that "if the executive is to secure their [the workers'] maximum energies and cooperation, there must be an understanding of the 'relativity' between different groups of workers . . . [because of] the workers' wish to enjoy social status through their job status."[11] Furthermore, Western Electric needed to improve communication with its employees and with the community. Williams recommended using *Western Electric News*, the company in-house magazine, to publicize workers' achievements, the activities of different departments and how they fit into the company's goals, information about company policies and plans, and the outlook for the future.

In 1923, Williams undertook two more studies at the request of the Western Electric Personnel Committee. The first involved operations in Cleveland, Chicago, Atlanta, and Hawthorne. Williams reported that of the four locations, the Chicago shop had the most problems with turnover, wage rates that were not comparable with prevailing area wages, and workers who did not receive adequate information about their performance and earnings records. The foremen needed to meet more frequently with upper-level management and should have more training in dealing with personnel problems. Williams found that morale was best in Atlanta, poorest in Cleveland, and "barely good" in Chicago.

Williams directed some special remarks at the Hawthorne plant. He felt that Hawthorne's public image could be improved if there were fewer security personnel at the gates and if the company used more dignified signs to indicate the route to the employment office. Internally, the Hawthorne plant needed to improve its communications with employees by using bulletin boards, slips in pay envelopes, and the company magazine to highlight human accomplishments and to inform workers of what happened to the products they made once the products left the factory. At Hawthorne, a practice existed called "button talks," in which higher-level executives circulated on the production floor to see, be seen, and talk with the workers. According to Williams, these button talks were received well by the workers and the practice should occur more often.

Furthermore, the Hawthorne plant needed to conduct a census of the different nationalities of its workers so that needs unique to their cultural backgrounds could be met more adequately. Another recommendation was that the Hawthorne plant needed to expand the training and development program for its foremen, the first line of supervision. Williams knew the importance of the first-line supervisor as the man in the middle between workers and management and, therefore, a vital link in communications and interpersonal relations. Recently, a longtime Hawthorne employee, Don Chipman, recalled what supervision was like in the early 1920s: "Supervision in those days was a different thing. . . . See, he [the supervisor] was the department head, and the department head was IT. He was the boss. He had the right to hire, fire, discipline in any manner he saw fit, and so forth and so on."[12] One of these foremen, Frank Platenka, was described as a person who relied upon fear to motivate employees, and one employee noted that Platenka was so mean that "[when] he died; I didn't even go to see him."[13] While Platenka was probably more of an exception than a rule, the foremen at Hawthorne definitely needed some "human skills."

Other recommendations that Williams made involved placing a woman on the Personnel Committee, centrally handling more personnel work, and improving lateral communications among departments. He noted that although Western Electric employed 10,000 females (roughly one-fourth of its employees), there was no female on the Personnel Committee. "Do not delay," he said, in placing a woman on the Personnel Committee. This was a rather radical proposal for the time, because women were not even eligible to be promoted to supervisory positions, much less to serve on a companywide personnel committee.[14] The centralization of personnel work would help all the departments. Williams also noted that different departments had poor lateral communications, which prevented the coordination of work efforts at the lowest possible levels.[15]

The rapid growth of Western Electric that had led to its need to improve its personnel policies and practices was largely due to the remarkable technological developments taking place at the time. In 1923, for example, Western Electric's vice-president for engineering, Frank B. Jewett, described what he called "Tele-Vision" and predicted that within ten years people would be able to "see the living image" simultaneously with the radio broadcast![16] Western Electric was also becoming a world leader in the communications field and had established plants in Great Britain and Europe to serve those markets.

Williams's second assignment, in 1923, was to study Western Electric's plants in Antwerp, Milan, London, and Paris. Williams found the physical working conditions at these plants to be above the average of other employers in these cities. Western Electric also paid higher wages, offered more regular employment, and was better able, therefore, to attract and keep better employees. The major problem in the European plants, according to Williams, involved the relationship between the American managers and their local subordinates. Evidently, there were few, if any, indigenous managers in these plants. Williams felt that a gap existed between workers and managers that was greater at the European plants than at any other place in the company. To resolve this problem, Williams did not recommend using more local managers but suggested training the existing supervisors how to deal more effectively and sensitively with these employees and using techniques to elicit ideas from the employees about their work.[17]

Williams's assignments in 1924 were focused on a program to train foremen. In numerous reports to the Personnel Committee, Williams had recommended training for the foremen in handling personnel matters. Western Electric did provide technical training and a general orientation program for newly hired college graduates who were expected to move into positions of greater responsibility.[18] Foremen, on the other hand, were selected and promoted from the ranks of lesser-skilled workers based on their display of technical, rather than managerial or human relations, skills. This did not mean that they were incompetent, but often they were not well prepared for the added responsibilities of a manager. Williams identified three objectives for Western Electric's supervisory training program: (1) to provide information about the company and the "materials, machines, and processes" it used; (2) to provide information about Western Electric and its industry; and (3) to provide instruction in "what a supervisor should know about his workers and the efficient direction of their energies."

As Williams had recommended, training classes for foremen began in 1924 with an emphasis on the "responsibilities of a foreman" and obtaining "effective production from jobs and men from the human angle."[19] Williams also had some advice for upper-level management on how to make this training effective. He said that higher-level managers should avoid giving the foremen the idea that there was an "official caste" in management and that to belong to this elite group, the foreman "must keep far away from his workers." If the foremen were led to believe that they were of the managerial "caste" and too far removed from the worker, "all [Western Electric] efforts to train the foreman in handling the workers are likely to be fruitless." Williams suggested that the foremen learn to avoid using fear as a motivator and learn to appeal to the workers' love of distinction as an incentive. Love of money was not an effective appeal; people wanted recognition and the lures of hope and pride in their work.[20]

A PRELUDE TO THE HAWTHORNE EXPERIMENTS. There is no record of any further consulting work at Western Electric by Williams after 1924. By the time he left, however, Western Electric was using the term "human relations" to refer to employee relations, and the company had, by any standard of the time, a very progressive set of personnel policies.[21] In 1924, Western Electric's Personnel Committee formulated nine policy statements that would be used to guide the relationship between management and the employees. Walter Dietz, secretary of the committee, drew them up; they were reviewed and approved by the committee and then presented to Charles Du Bois, the president. Mr. DuBois added a tenth policy and the list, which became known internally as the Ten Commandments, came into being:

    I. To pay all employees adequately for services rendered

    II. To maintain reasonable hours of work and safe working conditions

    III. To provide continuous employment consistent with business conditions

    IV. To place employees in the kind of work best suited to their abilities

    V. To help each individual to progress in the company's service

    VI. To aid employees in times of need

    VII. To encourage thrift

    VIII. To cooperate in social, athletic and other recreational activities

    IX. To accord to each employee the right to discuss freely with executives any matters concerning his or her welfare or the Company's interest

    X. To carry on the daily work in a spirit of friendliness[22]

These policies were developed and in place before the well-known Hawthorne experiments began, and they reflected the work of the Personnel Committee and its consultant, Whiting Williams. When Western Electric commemorated the fiftieth anniversary of the beginning of the Hawthorne studies, these Ten Commandments were still in place and serving the company and its employees.

The training program for foremen, which Williams had advocated, including managment training and instruction about the human angle, had been initiated in 1924 and was progressing through the company. Burleigh Gardner, a well-known social researcher, went to work for Western Electric as an employee counselor in 1936. Later he taught at the University of Chicago and wrote cogently about human relations in industry. By 1936, he recalled, Western Electric had a well-developed training program for foremen that far exceeded typical practices in other organizations: "After I left Western Electric I did a lot of research and consulting. I was constantly impressed by the competence of Western Electric foremen in dealing with human relations problems, as compared with foremen elsewhere. The roots of this must go back to the programs that Williams started."[23] Williams also had an impact on pay policies. A Hawthorne executive said, "Considerable importance is attached [at Hawthorne] to keeping labor grades on a proper basis with one another . . . so that the earnings of the unskilled operators will be in line with their training and experience."[24] This was recommended earlier by Williams and is another indication of his influence on Western Electric's personnel policies and practices.

In 1924, a series of experiments began, under the auspices of the National Research Council, to explore the relationship between the level of illumination in the workplace and worker productivity.[25] These experiments were abandoned by the illumination engineers when it was discovered that worker output increased over previous levels regardless of the level of illumination and certain other variables. It was George A. Pennock, the assistant works manager at Hawthorne, who insisted that the experiments be continued.

In 1927, Pennock, Homer Hibarger (of Western Electric), and Professor Clair E. Turner of the Massachusetts Institute of Technology began to manipulate other variables that could affect employee performance and attitudes. Later, Elton Mayo and other researchers became involved in what became famous as the Hawthorne experiments. These experiments led to the conclusions that supervisors needed to (1) develop their social skills; (2) reduce the social distance between themselves and their workers, who were "apprehensive of authority"; (3) develop listening skills and be open to and concerned with the problems of their workers; (4) pay less attention to money as an incentive and more to the workers' desire for group standing and approval; and (5) recognize that workers needed increased attention and would respond to a human-oriented style of supervision with improved morale and output.[26]

When Mary B. Gilson, another pioneer in labor-management

relations, reviewed the writings of the Hawthorne experimenters she stated that they could have saved years of effort if they had been acquainted with the "experiences of others."[27] While she did not name these "others," one of them was her old friend from Cleveland, Whiting Williams. In retrospect, it appears that the illumination study and the subsequent Hawthorne experiments never involved the Western Electric Personnel Committee. If later researchers had read the reports that Williams had provided to Mr. Halligan and the Personnel Committee, then the experiments might have taken on a different perspective.

Before the Hawthorne experiments began in 1924, the company had shown an interest in improving its personnel practices by employing Whiting Williams. Williams extended personnel work at Western Electric to interpersonal dealings, or human relations, between the management and the workers. It was Whiting Williams who had recommended: (1) supervisory training, especially in understanding of the human factor; (2) the hiring of interviewers to talk with those who were leaving the company to determine their reasons for leaving; (3) the idea that workers compared wages across similar skill levels; (4) the idea that job status was related to social status, hence that the factory was a social system; (5) the need for improved communication with the employees; (6) reducing the distance between manager and worker by disclaiming the idea that there was an "official caste" of managers; and (7) that workers responded to the appeal of distinction and recognition rather than fear. If one compares these findings with those of the Hawthorne experimenters, it is apparent that Williams anticipated many of their findings. In the reports of Whiting Williams can be found a prelude to the Hawthorne experiments, the beginning of developing ideas about how labor-management relations could be improved through better human understanding.

In summary, Williams turned his investigative skills and his "old clothes" appearance into a successful practice as a counselor to industry. He worked with top management, advising on how both physical and human working conditions could be improved. He worked for a notable group of employers over the years, an indication that his abilities were recognized as beneficial to progressive companies that wished to improve their labor-management relations. Finally, he recommended numerous new policies and practices at the Western Electric Company, which provided a prelude to later research about human relations in industry.

The Mainsprings of Men

IN ADDITION to his travels, consulting service, and writings, Williams also led an active life as a teacher and lecturer. In his speeches to various groups and in various classrooms, he told many listeners of his experiences as a worker and of what he had learned about ways to improve employee-employer relations. He spoke to community groups, trade associations, and groups of practicing business executives who had the opportunity to put his ideas into practice. There was yet another group of listeners he addressed as "the new leaders," those who were still in college and preparing to be the managers of the future. Williams hoped his appearances at Dartmouth, Harvard, Northwestern, and other business schools would reach these future executives and influence the direction they would take as "industrial statesmen."

Teaching and Lecturing

While the Wharton School of Finance and Commerce at the University of Pennsylvania was America's first successful undergraduate school of business, the continued growth of America's businesses required even more advanced preparation in business affairs. The Amos Tuck School of Administration and Finance at Dartmouth College was founded in 1900, making it America's first graduate school of business administration. The second graduate school of business was founded in 1908 at Harvard University.[1] It was at Dartmouth and Harvard that graduate education for business began, and each school was expected to be on the leading edge of knowledge related to business practice. Since interest was high in the rapidly developing field of personnel and labor relations, and since Williams had published his highly successful report of living and working with the workers, *What's On the Worker's Mind?* it was not long before he was asked to appear as a lecturer. Williams was appointed a lecturer on labor problems at Harvard in 1920, and he presented five-week courses to Harvard's business policy and/or industrial management classes from 1920 through 1928 and from 1936 through 1941.[2]

Under its first dean, Edwin F. Gay, the Harvard Business School had emphasized the use of instructors and lecturers from outside the academic world. Because of the gap that existed between business practice and academic life at the time, Gay felt that outsiders, including scientific management pioneers Frederick W. Taylor and Carl Barth, were essential to helping the business school fit its role of preparing people for business practice. Wallace Brett Donham, Gay's successor as dean in 1919, continued this practice but placed less emphasis on outside lecturers as the years went by.[3]

There was concern in the business community not only about what was taught in the business school but also about who was teaching or lecturing on various subjects. Howard Elliott, a member of the business school's board of overseers, wrote to Dean Donham that the school had a "reputation for socialism, bolshevism, etc." and that a planned fund-raising campaign would be more successful "if we were in a position to say that a man like Mr. Fechner [who represented the viewpoint of organized labor at the business school] . . . was not employed by the college."[4] Donham defended Fechner as "an exceedingly valuable member of our staff," but Elliott and the board of overseers were not entirely satisfied and requested information about other lecturers at the school; one of these special inquiries was about Whiting Williams. Williams did not appear to represent organized labor's point of view, but he did lecture about labor relations, and this evidently raised some doubts among the overseers. Donham replied to the board of overseers that

> Mr. Williams was formerly labor vice president and employment manager of the Hydraulic Pressed Steel Company in Cleveland and for the last two years has been spending all his time studying, speaking and writing on the labor situation. He has made a study of it in this country, England, France, to some extent Germany, and this summer is going to Spain and Italy. You may have read some of his magazine articles or his books "What's on the Worker's Mind" and "Full Up and Fed Up."[5]

The board of overseers apparently became satisfied that Williams was not a radical, for no other questions arose about his yearly lectures at the business school. Professor Washburn, of the business school, praised Williams to Dean Donham in this memo:

> *Industrial Management, Mr. Whiting Williams, 11-12:* This
> seems to be a very popular lecture and included the whole first
> year class. Mr. Williams had himself been in the gangs in the
> different industries that he alluded to and the time was taken up
> largely by reciting the relations of foremen to their men and
> largely by indicating what they should not be.[6]

Dean Donham also recommended Williams to the dean of Harvard's
Engineering School as one "who does a very effective piece of work
for us every year on the human side of management problems."[7]

Although Dean Donham relied less and less on outside lecturers,
one of those who returned many times was Whiting Williams. The
topics that Williams addressed varied from year to year; they included
"A Problem in Labor Relations" (1922–1923); "Labor's Point of
View" (1923–1924); "Morale at Excelsior Steel" (1924–1925 and
1925–1926); "The Human Factor for Executives" (1926–1927); and
"The Executive as Creator of Organizational Energy" (1927–1928).[8]
Williams told his business policy class that the study of business policy was "inadequate" without an understanding of "people working in
a framework of relationships." To develop as a manager, a person
needed to "know the power of facts," the "power of feelings," and the
"factual importance of feelings."[9] These "new leaders" needed to
bring the feelings of their employees into the decision-making process, which should be based not strictly on facts, but on facts as influenced by feelings. Harvard's president Charles W. Eliot invited
Williams to his home to "explain his ideas," and Williams enjoyed a
successful series of lectures over many years at one of America's leading educational institutions.[10]

Williams began his five-week courses in human relations at the
Amos Tuck School at Dartmouth in 1921 and they continued annually
until 1941. The lectures were essentially identical to those given at
Harvard for any given year and maintained certain themes such as
unemployment, the role of the foreman, the status of workers, how
radicals appealed to laboring people, how unions were organized, and
so forth.[11] One student who attended Williams's classes at Dartmouth
recalled him as "a university lecturer of almost glamourous distinction" whose conferences at Dartmouth and Harvard "pointed up the
academic year in New England." As Williams entered, the student
recalled, he was trailed by half a dozen chattering professors "who
came with the students to hear this noted lecturer."[12] Ernest Hopkins,
Dartmouth's president, wrote praises of *What's On the Worker's*

Mind?, invited Williams back to lecture again, and served as a reference for him on his various jaunts.[13] At the graduate business schools at Harvard and Dartmouth, where he made his most frequent appearances, Williams was reaching the future leaders he sought to influence with his observations about work, workers, and managers.

Williams did not confine his interest in future business leaders to Dartmouth and Harvard. Through his various contacts with labor leaders, business leaders, and academicians, he often was asked to speak to other groups. One interesting anecdote has been provided by James C. Worthy, a successful man in business, government, and academia who came into contact with Whiting Williams at Northwestern University in the 1930s. As an undergraduate at Northwestern, Dr. Worthy was one of a select group of students who had been named Austin Scholars and given a particularly innovative educational regimen. The faculty sponsor of the group was Earl Dean Howard, professor of Economics at Northwestern and vice-president for labor relations at Hart, Schaffner, and Marx, the clothiers. Howard had played a key role in the Rochester Plan, which was the clothing industry's counterpart to the B&O Plan, one of William's favorite themes. Thus, this relationship between Professor Howard and Williams was used to benefit the Austin Scholar Program. Dr. Worthy recalled that

> one of the things that Howard did was have the scholars spend Thursday evenings the greater part of each school year at his home, where Mrs. Howard served us apple juice and cookies. These sessions carried no academic credit, but in many ways they were the highlight of the entire Austin Scholarship program.
>
> Howard frequently had special guests in to meet and talk with students. Usually, these were businessmen, and we had the opportunity to meet and get to know personally a fair number of the top business leaders of the day.
>
> One of the guests whom I remember particularly well was Whiting Williams. He was present at perhaps five or six meetings during the years 1930–31. His special topic always had something to do with what workers were like, what they thought about their jobs and their bosses, and how they reacted to the kinds of things their bosses and their companies did to them. He always spoke from first-hand knowledge because when doing his field work he made it a practice to dress and act like a worker and whenever possible—which apparently was fairly often—to get jobs and work along-side bona fide workmen. I remember particularly his talking about miners and mine work, and about steel workers and steel mills.
>
> Williams was not a vivid personality but he captured the

interest and imagination of his listeners; we always looked forward to the evenings we knew he would be present. Most of the students were from small towns or rural areas and had little exposure to the kinds of working situations Williams talked about.

He had the ability to make the people and circumstances he described come alive, and we found it easy to put ourselves in their place and to see things as they saw them. Williams related very well to the students, as I am sure he did to the workers whose lives and work he studied. He answered questions readily and fully, never showed any sign of impatience, and seemed to thoroughly enjoy being with us. He conveyed to us his enthusiasm for his subject, and our meetings with him always outlasted their scheduled time.

As I remember him, he was not exactly shabbily dressed but he certainly didn't have the sartorial polish of the big businessmen with whom we also met. In cold weather, he would arrive at the Howard home in a rather beat-up, gray felt hat with a turned-up rim, and in an overcoat that could not have been a recent purchase; personal attire obviously did not rank high among his priorities. That didn't bother us at all; we were much more interested in what he had to say than in what he happened to wear.

Looking back more than fifty years later I remember most the man and only dimly the things he talked about. In retrospect, I think he must at least have laid the groundwork in our minds for what later became known as "human relations." At least, so far as am concerned, when I began to read Mayo and Roethlisberger and Dickson I felt I was in territory not altogether unfamiliar . . . looking back I think I have been more influenced by him than I may have realized.[14]

Williams became such a popular speaker that he employed an agent to make the necessary arrangements and to set up the schedules. For example, between 1919 and 1923 he addressed over 125 groups from Maine to California at a typical fee of $100 per speech plus expenses.[15] His message was being widely and well received, but in addition to these successes he felt he needed to distill his experiences and ideas into another book.

The Wish for Worth

Williams's first three books were reports, extensions of the diaries he kept while on the road and leading his double life. From his experiences in teaching at Dartmouth, Harvard, and Northwestern and from his lectures, however, Williams perceived a need to bring together his travels, experiences, and observations into a textbook. He felt that "men were searching for the springs of action within themselves and within their fellows" and he hoped his text would "furnish to such seekers a few suggestions capable of daily application."[16] In order to facilitate this emphasis on practice and application, Williams chose to use the "case or problem method . . . as it has been used in the class-rooms of the Graduate Schools of Business at Dartmouth and Harvard where for several years it has been a privilege to discuss the content of these chapters."[17] The book that came out of these goals was *The Mainsprings of Men* which, broadly conceived, dealt with the subjects of motivation and leadership.

The "mainsprings" that Williams explored involved questions about the prime moving forces—the things, events, desires, and experiences—that caused people to seek and to do what they did. His conclusions came from his observations of workers, the numerous talks he had with people in different countries and different occupations, and his own reflections on these experiences.

Although it was believed by many that workers were basically lazy and preferred easy jobs, Williams had found just the reverse!

> From my contacts with the earners of salaries, as well as of wages, I would venture to assert that while some unhappiness and bitterness exists because too much is being required of the workers, an enormously greater volume of discontent and disappointment results because the members of our commercial and industrial organizations, from top to bottom, are being regularly asked to give LESS than they would like to give. Most employers think they can make work acceptable if they make it merely easy![18]

These defective assumptions about people and the nature of work, according to Williams, could be traced to the then popular notions of human motivation, in particular, instinct theory.

A common theme at this time was that people were animated by instincts: Thorstein Veblen, an economist; William James, a philosopher; and Ordway Tead, a personnel psychologist, are among those who concluded that instincts such as workmanship, play, curiosity, pugnacity, and a host of others explained our behavior.[19] Williams repudiated instinct theories, claiming that the lists grew longer and longer without general agreement. Furthermore, the instincts that guided some people did not apply to all others: "The very number of all these action-triggers makes them cumbersome for the manager of men."[20] Williams recognized that any general ideas about motivation would overlook individual differences; conversely, to focus on an individual might not enable generalizations to be made about others: "It is likely that no concise statement can adequately define the full force and direction of all our human appetites and yearnings. Nevertheless, there is need of . . . naming some [motives] which may help anyone who cares to touch the aspirations or the energies of his fellows."[21]

The one factor that helped most to explain motivation, according to Williams, was "our wish to enjoy the feeling of our worth as persons among other persons. This feeling can hardly exist without a corresponding recognition and respect on the part of others."[22] Williams supported these needs people had for respect and recognition by quoting from his vast reservoir of conversations with his fellow workers:

> [George, an electrician] Well, I was eighteen and had no trade in a little Iowa town, so I joined the navy. Here's my certificate — "First-class electrician." See? And in those four years I saw almost the whole world. You bet it takes the juice to run a cruiser — a big generator to turn every turret besides all the other things. Now I get good money, eight-hour day and interesting work.
>
> [Elizabeth, a worker in the information booth in a railway station] Polite? Well, I'll tell the world people ain't polite to us girls! No, we never get any thanks, and lotsa time they tell us, "Well it was five-ten and not five-fifteen yesterday, 'cause I looked at my watch." And all the fool things they expect us to know and get sore if we don't! ("Yes, sir, one at five-forty and another at five-fifty-five.") We get some training inside answering the 'phone. ("Blankburg? — track 4, madam.") Oh, I've wanted to hang up on 'em many's the time.[23]

This mainspring, this wish for enjoying a feeling of worth as a person, made people more responsive to social than to psychological or economic inducements. With this wish for worth as the polestar of human activity, it would be easier to explain the constellation of other things that affected our behavior. For example, Williams came close to developing a theory of a hierarchy of human needs: "The farther the worker's skill takes him away from the hunger minimum, the more his pay-check's ability to buy material things is overshadowed by its ability to purchase an immaterial something of equal importance and vastly greater intricacy . . . his standing as a worker among his fellow workers."[24]

In Williams's view, certain basic needs existed that had to be met (for example, hunger) but once these needs were fulfilled, other things became more important to a person as he or she moved toward a feeling of worth. This feeling of worth involved a need to belong as well as a need to enjoy the recognition and esteem of others. Physical working conditions were important and helped to determine the factors of "skill, craftmanship, freedom from supervision, the direction of great power [for example, machinery] or other workers, responsibility of every sort, opportunity for promotion, and protection against discharge or lay off," all of which were items that workers used in their comparisons of the standing of one job to other jobs.[25]

How much a person earned was important in a relation to how much others earned. Beyond the basic wages necessary to survival, people compared their earnings to those of others within the job hierarchy. Williams illustrated this point with two stories, one from the railway strike of 1922 and one from a British worker:

> The trouble came [the head of a railroad brotherhood explained] from certain inexperienced war-time officials. They did not know how all of us railroaders had, in the course of years, finally worked out our places in the railway scale of wages so that we all knew where we stood in the line without being eternally sore at each other. For instance, the "car-knocker," or repairer, was for years perfectly content to get, say, a "differential" of five cents an hour less than a "shack," or brakeman. Then in that whole department, the machinist, the blacksmith, the sheet-metal worker and others expected to get just so many cents more or less than the car-knocker. Likewise the conductor was satisfied to get, say, a dollar a day more than the brakeman. So when these government officials calmly proceeded to give the "car-knocker" five cents an hour more than a brakeman, the whole wage system of the country's roads was just about turned upside down! . . . Not for a moment can a single one of all these men forget the butcher's or the baker's bills but as long as every one of these earners is human, it is equally impossible for a single one of them to forget his place in the line in comparison with every other railway-worker of every other kind and category between the Atlantic and the Pacific![26]
>
> The raises ain't been fair [the Newcastle machinist argued]. Now, 'ere's my 'elper. All the war awards 'as raised 'im 195 per cent above pre-war, w'ilst they've raised me only 125 per cent. Thot makes 'im draw almost the same as me. But if any job's wrong, it's me that gets all the blame, not 'im. Now, thot's wrong! And then 'ere's these dockers and all sorts of general laborers besides. No six or seven years of apprenticin' for them, d'ye understand? — but still a-gettin' their sixteen bob a day! Thot's wrong, all wrong![27]

These examples indicated that workers became unhappy when the pay structure became out of line with the workers' perceptions of the hierarchy of jobs. While earnings were important, they acted primarily as carriers of social worth in the eyes of the worker.

Job status also determined social status because "everywhere among the workers a man determines the social standing of himself and his family, not so much by the earning power as by the NATURE of his job."[28] While men determined their status and the status of their families by their jobs, this was not true with female workers. In Williams's opinion,

> While [the] wife's social standing similarly depends mainly on [her] husband's occupation, her unmarried sister is much more likely to consider her paid job not so much as a career in itself as an aid to her enjoyment of the "honorable estate" of matrimony. "Believe me," so replied the young lady clerk in a department store to the proposal that she join a class on salesmanship, "my future don't lie on no panty-counter!"[29]

Furthermore, Williams stated, "A woman's interest in her plant or office career tends to vary inversely with the square of her interest in matrimony."[30] While Williams would be judged a male chauvinist by today's standards, his opinion of women at work represented the prevailing social values of the period in which he wrote. Some Victorian values about the role of women in society still lingered. To his credit, Williams did note some trends that would eventually put more women in the work force. These included increasing numbers of women receiving higher educations, more laborsaving devices for the home, more women in the professions, and more women returning to work soon after marriage to supplement the family finances. Nevertheless, it was apparent that Williams was concerned that the woman at work would lose sight of her societal role as the focal point of the family.[31]

While women did not measure their worth by their work, according to Williams, one of the first questions asked about a man in almost any type of new situation or conversation was "What does he do?"[32] This question was asked in order to place the man in the social hierarchy because "it is impossible to judge the effect of either wage or other conditions of work apart from the relationships the work permits with other persons. What every worker knows is this: that sooner or later the final joy of his work is settled, not by him nor by his employer, but by the social standing awarded him by his fellow citizens."[33] What the worker did inside the workplace affected how he or she and his or her family stood in the community; similarly, problems in the community could be brought back into the workplace by the worker. "This vital connection between job status and social status means that the problem of effective relations with the worker inside the factory cannot be successfully separated from the whole problem of general social relations outside [the factory]."[34] This view of the place of work as part of a broader social system put Williams in advance of other theories about humankind and the importance of work. Williams quoted from Dostoevsky's *The House of the Dead* to illustrate this point: "If it were desired to reduce a man to nothing, to punish him atrociously, to crush him in such a manner that the most hardened murderer would tremble before such punishment — it would be necessary only to give his work a character of complete uselessness."[35]

Williams gave numerous examples to support his view that work was part of the mainspring of a feeling of worthiness. "Pride in work" was the key phrase he used to describe how workers wanted to be seen as important in a larger scheme of things. One of Williams's favorite stories about how workers wished to feel worthy involved a Welsh coal miner: "Wull, it been plain to see," so old Evan, the repairman in Rhondda Valley mine would call back to me when, tools on shoulder and lamp in hand, we would start for our next chore after we had cleared the rails of the fall of rock and thus permitted the colliers or coal miners to continue loading their cars, "it been plain to see, they cawn't run the bloody mine — nor all the shops and factories oop outside — without you and me!"[36]

Another favorite was one he borrowed from Daniel Willard and involved how the worker, despite the hierarchy of managers, was still the one who finally got the job done. "Last week," so Pietro explained why he was tamping the tie,

> last week when President he come over dees joint here, hees special car go "Boomp." So he ask Beeg Engineer, next chair, "Say, why dat boomp?" Engineer he tell Divis' Sup'tendent, next chair, "Hey! Better Feex!" And Sup'tendent ask Divis' Engineer, next chair, "Say, how soon feex boomp!" Last night Track Boss call up my boss and holler, "Whyda hell not feex boomp, huh?" Deesa morning my boss he tell me, "Hey, Pete, feex boomp — Goddam quick!" Me feexa da bump![37]

Workers wanted to feel pride, but sometimes they also felt the need for social activities on the job. Williams observed that workers often resisted attempts to reduce monotony and to make their work more interesting because they liked the routine, which became a habit that allowed them time to socialize with others or to daydream. "Whatever its cause," noted Williams,

> this general acceptance of monotonous work supplies at least one reason why plant superintendents report that so many workers steadfastly refuse the proffered change to "more interesting" operations. In one great automobile factory famous for the monotony of its tasks, an order to "change everybody's job where possible every six months" all but produced a riot, and had to be withdrawn![38]

Pride in work could still be found in factory jobs even though the division of labor among workers had led to increasingly specialized tasks. While some hailed the "old days," that is, the times before the Industrial Revolution and the factory system, as the golden age of craftsmanship, Williams argued that the ancient crafts were most often highly specialized also. For example, a knife or other cutting instrument was made not by one craftsman, but by three: the "cutlers" made the handle; the "bladesmiths" the blade; and the sheath was made by "sheathers." Thus, even these crafts divided labor and each worker did less than the whole job. While we praise craftsmanship, the real joy in work is in the creation of something that is useful to other people. According to Williams,

> the craftsman of an earlier day probably got less pleasure than we assume out of making the whole of his wagon. Certainly he had no chance to be bored: almost each day brought some fresh problem, or demanded some fresh skill. Nevertheless, when he saw his finished work before him, his joy of creation was less the joy of creating a thing than a *service*. So his delight came not so much from making the whole of his product, as from keeping in touch with it after it changed from a thing to a service, and thus began its active usefulness. His thrill of craftsmanship thus resulted not so much from the conditions of his job as from those of his market — a market which made the user of his handiwork a neighbor.[39]

This pride of craftsmanship was still available to those who were able to relate their part, however small, to the creation of the whole product or service.

In brief, Williams's experiences and observations had led him to reject instinct theory, the prevailing notion of motivation, as defective because it did not account for human variability and left the manager with an inadequate idea of people's needs. People had numerous needs, ranging from very basic to very complex ones of job status, social status, and pride in work. People wanted to be recognized and respected for what they did. The wish for worth was the mainspring of men, "For in our work . . . we hope to become a person who is meaningful and valuable—aye, indispensable—to others!"[40] The wish for worth animated us to seek fulfilling jobs, to be members in good standing among our fellows, to be insecure and fearful if threatened, and to say the workers' prayer, "Give us this day our daily job."

Leadership Skills for Managers

The identification of the mainsprings of men would be of little value unless this understanding was transmitted to managers for their use in developing better relations with their employees: "In none of us is the mainspring broken: only its control, its escapement, is faulty. The meaning of this for the would-be leader of men is evident. How best to touch those mainsprings and release their abundant powers into the desired channels?"[41]

One way of developing this understanding would be in on-the-job supervisory development programs in industry, such as the ones Williams recommended at Western Electric; another would be in the new business schools, such as those at Dartmouth and Harvard, where the leaders of the future were being prepared. In any situation, managers, especially the first-line supervisors, were a connecting link between the worker and the job. When Williams asked a group of workers which they preferred, "a good foreman and a lousy job, or a good job with a lousy foreman? [they responded] 'Of all the damn-fool questions that is the damn-foolest. There is no such thing as a good job and a lousy foreman, there is no such thing as a lousy job with a good foreman.'"[42]

The relationship between the manager and the worker thus became critical in determining how the worker felt about himself and others. Williams stressed what he called the "leadership of cooperation," which required that managers obey the Eleventh Commandment ("Thou shalt not take thy neighbor for granted"), which could be put into practice by explaining to workers where their work fit into the total, appealing to hope rather than to fear, and providing for two-way communications between managers and workers. The first-line supervisor was the man in the middle and was essential to the linkage of management to the workers:

The foreman is best fitted by his position to facilitate the movement of information in two directions — to pass instructions and
facts to his workers, and also to know and report their changing
moods and interests. Nevertheless, it will always be extremely
difficult to get the foreman to meet the pressure for maximum
output placed upon him by his superior, and at the same time get
and pass on to the same superior a frank expression of viewpoint obtained from close and friendly contact with his workers.
Such a combination remains well-nigh impossible until the leader
is so trained that his promise of reward secures larger results
from his followers than does any amount of the old threats or
pressures. It should be said, however, that in some plants the
foreman does a better job of instructing and leading his men than
does his superintendent in instructing or leading him![43]

Thus, the first-line supervisor was the contact point for labor and
management, and how that supervisor behaved and treated his or her
workers would be crucial to organizational success. For example, by
listening to the workers, first-line supervisors could identify and treat
complaints before they became grievances, elicit ideas about perform-
ing the job better, and pay attention to the workers instead of passing
them by as if they were part of the machinery.

The type of leadership that was needed, in Williams's view, was
lacking in most managers at that time. One of the few exceptions was
Daniel Willard, whom Williams felt personified the type of leadership
needed in business. Willard's philosophy was a model for all:

We aim to give to every employee an enlightened and enlarged
view of his own worth and importance as a part of our great
organization. We emphasize to each man the importance of the
work which he himself is doing, and the responsibility which goes
with his job or position, and which rests upon him personally to
do good work . . . not just because it is really his duty as an
honest man to give good work in return for good wages paid in
good money, but because, realizing the responsibility which he
shares with the management for the safe and proper operation of
the railroad, he *wants* to do good work. . . . So it has come
about that the workmen themselves in greater degree than ever
before are doing, and doing happily, the best that is in them, not
just because they feel they are *obliged* to do it, but rather because
they *want* to do it.[44]

Such a philosophy at the top of the organization provided an example
for others throughout the organization. The future of industry rested
in the hands of those who were willing and able to practice this new

philosophy of leadership. The new leaders would be developed in the newly emerging business schools and in training programs for supervisors who were already at work in industry. The case problems that Williams provided in his text, *Mainsprings of Men*, demonstrated how he wished to develop these leadership skills by emphasizing practical situations. There were usually ten or more "problems" at the end of each chapter. The following two provide examples of the situations he posed for classroom problem solving and discussion:

> Suppose the following statements of the workers in a spinning mill are brought to your attention: "You need strong legs and no brains for this work"; "You think about other things"; "Piecers get disgusted—they are always getting disgusted"; "It's the walking and the breaking threads"; As an executive would you be satisfied to let these conditions remain as they are? What do the workers' statements point to? Do they have any pride in their work? How would you handle the situation?
>
> A foreman found it frequently necessary to criticise the work and general demeanor of a lathe operator in a metal-working plant. The workman interpreted the criticism as indicating personal animosity. He thought the foreman "had it in for him," and was trying to make things unpleasant for him so he would leave. The foreman found he must speak to him again for the slovenly appearance of his machine, and for impertinence to the assistant foreman, who called the operator's attention to the machine's condition. How should the foreman make the criticism? What suggestions would you have made to him in order to overcome the worker's obsession that the foreman was trying to "get him?"[45]

While supervisors on the front line of labor-management relations needed to develop and/or improve their skills in dealing with workers, the example needed to be set at the top of the organization. Here Williams emphasized the role played by example and demonstration. First-line managers would be sorely restricted if their supervisors wished for them to cling to previous methods of managing workers. Since Williams's consulting assignments had brought him into contact with upper-level executives, he knew the importance of these people as business statesmen who should set "high ethical standards and have positive attitudes about serving the public."[46] In these executive positions, decisions had a more far-reaching impact on economics and human lives than might the decisions of a ruler of a foreign country. Therefore, the executives of these corporate institutions needed broad training, perspective, high ideals, and the vision of statesmen. Under this new leadership, labor and management could "think together, feel together, and grow together" because each, through greater understanding, would share information, stabilize employment, use participative schemes such as shop councils, and recognize that they had mutual interests in working together.

The 1920s: A Reflection

When Whiting Williams and others looked back upon the decade of the 1920s they liked what they saw. In the immediate aftermath of a great war there had been strikes, other manifestations of industrial unrest, unemployment, inflation, fear of revolution, and a host of other indications of social and industrial divisiveness. Throughout the 1920s, however, the changes had been so dramatic that the period became known as the "prosperity decade." Unemployment never rose above 5 percent, the number and severity of strikes diminished, wages and real wages rose, price stability was achieved, and American unionism developed a character that was businesslike rather than radical.

The progress in labor-management relations during the 1920s led to lower labor turnover, improved morale, stable employment, and higher productivity.[47] Labor and management cooperated with each other; shop councils gave workers a role in decisions that affected their welfare; employee stock ownership became more widespread; pension benefits and insurance plans for health and life were added to protect the worker; and employers showed more concern for their employees. Williams noted these developments and used the phrase "human resources" to refer to an organization's employees because they represented an investment just as would any other asset of the firm. There were no "cookbook answers to human relations" problems and managers must think of the "total situation" when dealing with people.[48] Employers evidenced a greater concern for their employees, and labor responded. If mutual understanding is the key to mutual progress, the white collar hobo played his role in explaining the worker to management and management to the worker and in helping to bridge any distance that existed between these two parties in industrial situations.

SEVEN

The Dark Years

THE PROSPEROUS DECADE of the 1920s was followed by a decade of economic depression, social turbulence, and political upheaval for the American nation. The depression would spread worldwide, fascism would flourish in Germany and Italy, and the threat of an overthrow of society by radicals would again be present. Organized labor, relatively dormant during the 1920s, would gain greater leverage with the coming of the political regime of President Franklin D. Roosevelt. For Whiting Williams, the decade of the 1930s also brought personal tragedy and heartbreak.

Hard Times

October 29, 1929, is known in American economic history as "Black Tuesday." On that day, the stock market declined and wiped out $14 billion in stock values. By November 13, 1929, the total would be $30 billion, and for more than a decade all of American life was to be substantially changed by the stock market crash that preceded the Great Depression. In 1929, 48 million persons were employed while only about 1.5 million persons were unemployed (Table 7.1). Unemployment would rise, however, peaking at 12,830,000 unemployed (24.9 percent of the work force) in 1933. The number of unemployed would drop below 8 million only once thereafter in that decade—in 1937 when the number was 7,700,000 (14.3 percent of the work force).

Williams must have had a feeling of déjà vu, for he had stood in the job lines of 1919 and written of the economic, social, and spiritual heartbreak of unemployment during the 1921 recession. It was time again for Williams to take off his white collar shirt and to put back on

TABLE 7.1. Unemployment: 1929–1939 (annual averages)

Year	Number Unemployed	Unemployed as Percentage of Total Labor Force
1929	1,550,000	3.2
1930	4,340,000	8.7
1931	8,020,000	15.9
1932	12,060,000	23.6
1933	12,830,000	24.9
1934	11,340,000	21.7
1935	10,610,000	20.1
1936	9,030,000	16.9
1937	7,700,000	14.3
1938	10,390,000	19.0
1939	9,480,000	17.2

Source: U.S. Bureau of the Census, *Historical Statistics of the United States: Colonial Times to 1970* (Washington, D.C.: U.S. Government Printing Office, 1975), pt. 1, p. 135. These figures are annual averages that level out seasonal fluctuations. One labor economist has estimated that the actual peak of unemployment (that is, without averaging) was 30 percent in 1933. *See* Lloyd G. Reynolds, *Labor Economics and Labor Relations,* 4th ed. (Englewood Cliffs, N.J.: Prentice-Hall, 1964), p. 339.

his hobo clothes to hit the road and see the impact of these hard times from the viewpoint of the worker. In the summers of 1930, 1931, and 1932 he stood again in the unemployment lines, talked with relief recipients, and interviewed a variety of workers, union officials, and managers.

The first thing that struck Williams was that there were substantial differences between the unemployment he had seen in 1921 and what he observed as one of the unemployed in the summer of 1930. One of these differences was an improved relationship between labor and management, which had responded to President Hoover's call for work-sharing. In November 1929, President Hoover had asked for labor-management cooperation in reducing hours of work per worker per week as an alternative to laying off workers. Williams found that employers were responding to this plea and that work-sharing was successful. The workers' total weekly wages were reduced, but this was better than no work at all. Williams also found that when employers reduced the hours of work, they typically did not reduce the wage rate per hour, as had been the practice during 1921. Williams's favorite model of what a business leader should be, Daniel Willard, cut his own salary from $150,000 to $60,000 per year as an example of sacrifice when the railroad managements were requesting a 10 percent wage reduction from the railroad unions.[1]

In addition to positive responses from labor and management to work-sharing and to sharing the burdens of the economic downturn,

Williams also noted that the workers had a better cushion against the decline. This cushion had been built from the progressive labor policies of management during the 1920s; employer-sponsored thrift plans, for instance, gave workers savings to fall back upon, and more workers owned their homes than ever before because they had been able to save for the investment. Employee stock ownership had been a mixed blessing: as stock prices soared in the late 1920s some employees had sold their stock and entered into the general orgy of stock market speculation only to regret this decision later; other employees had kept their stocks only to see them plummet in 1929, still with regret. Intended to give the workers a share in the company, these plans proved that some modifications would have to be made to protect these stocks from severe ups and downs of the market. Williams also noted a change in attitudes about women working outside the home. From economic necessity, women were entering the labor force to try to bolster family income.

Finally, evidence of the most dramatic difference between previous years and 1930 was that the workers used their automobiles to look for work! Before, Williams had "hoofed" or "hitched" his way from one unemployment line to another—in 1930, the workers took their "Flivver." Williams commented that the entire family was working as much as possible in order "to play its proper part in that well-known indoor and outdoor American sport of keeping the wolf away from the garage door! The depression proves that the American wage earner has come to feel definitely that his self-respect and his standing among his neighbors require not only the roof above his head, but also the gas pedal beneath his feet."[2] Or, as the humorist Will Rogers noted: "We are the first nation in the history of the world to go to the poor house in an automobile."[3]

Williams's 1930 hobo trek had included Chicago, Detroit, Cleveland, Gary, and Pittsburgh. In the summer of 1931, Williams headed out again, "with a blue shirt, square chin, and a six-day beard" to revisit the above cities, as well as to explore South Bend, Columbus, and Cincinnati. The results in 1931 were not uplifting; the hard times had hit even the most frugal, industrious, and "sober" citizens. Hardest hit were towns that were heavily dependent on one type of industry, such as steel or coal. Williams also noted that racial prejudice was causing hardships: in Cincinnati, he remarked, 10 percent of the population was black, but blacks represented 45 percent of those on relief. Also disproportionately affected were unskilled workers and immigrants. Williams commented that a whole generation would bear a "social scar" from the self-worth lost through unemployment. Ramifications would include women taking jobs to help their families, and children being pulled out of school to go to work.[4] His prediction proved right. Some forty years later another student of work, Studs Terkel, obtained an oral history of the depression by interviewing those who had felt the impact of "hard times." Terkel summed up the effect of unemployment on those who remembered the depression: "The suddenly-idle hands blamed themselves, not society . . . the millions experienced a private kind of shame when the pink slip [layoff or discharge notice] came. No matter that others suffered the same fate, the inner voice whispered, 'I'm a failure!'"[5] Williams, who saw the spiritual side of unemployment, used different words forty years earlier, but his sentiments were the same.

While widespread unemployment led to economic losses, just as painful were loss of pride and self-esteem. This was Williams's recurring theme—that work is central to one's standing in the community. "There is no substitute whatsoever for a job—except another job."[6] Relief doles did not solve the problem, they merely postponed it. Williams continued his opposition to unemployment insurance, expect as a temporary measure to alleviate the problem while the economy and business were able to recover. "Security," as practiced in Great Britain and Europe, "was entirely too high a price in terms of worker opportunity."[7]

Williams clung to his belief that the answer to the depression resided in stimulating business and, in the short run, depending upon "coordinated benevolence" in the cities, counties, and states. In an interview on nationwide NBC radio during the depths of the depression, Williams opposed federal public works to relieve unemployment. He saw them as a device to transfer, rather than to solve, the problem, because the government had to take the money from taxpayers and savers, thus reducing their spending power to increase that of others.

The proper solution, he maintained, was the creation of jobs in the private sector of the economy.[8] This had worked in 1921, and there was no reason to believe that it would not work again. To provide local initiatives, as in 1921, President Hoover formed the President's Organization on Unemployment Relief under the direction of Walter S. Gifford, president of American Telephone and Telegraph (AT&T). While Gifford maintained that local initiative could provide the relief, Allen Burns, director of the American Association of Community Chests and Councils, said that local action would not be enough. While America's 200 local community chest associations had raised over $67 million in 1931, they needed at least $100 million for 1932.[9] This was the struggle, put simply and directly, as America was on the eve of an election: could America depend on self-help and local initiative as it had done in the past, or had the problem become so great that federal action was needed?

In this election year, in addition to the candidates Hoover for the Republicans and Franklin D. Roosevelt for the Democrats, America was presented with the possibility of some radical candidates: the Communist party nominated William Z. Foster for president and the Socialists nominated Norman Thomas. Williams favored the incumbent, Herbert Hoover, because "he [Hoover] understands current government and business problems better than any other candidate . . . and like a true Quaker engineer, he figures it is better for the driver to keep busy in his cab rather than to pass out cigars in the coaches."[10] To test the political winds, Williams took to the streets again in the summer of 1932, "waiting outside employment offices, sleeping in the ten-cent all night movie houses of Detroit or in the parks of Chicago, and helping hoboes boil out their socks in a tin can."[11] Williams found that the workers were not responding to agitators and predicted, quite accurately, that the radical candidates would make a poor showing despite their glowing promises. Out of a total vote of 40 million, Foster received 102,000 votes, while the Socialist candidate, Thomas, garnered fewer votes than the 919,000 that Eugene Debs had received in 1920. Of course, Williams's favorite, Hoover, fell to the newcomer, Franklin Delano Roosevelt.

In his acceptance speech for the Democratic party nomination, Roosevelt had said, "I pledge you, I pledge myself, to a New Deal for the American people." This pledge became the slogan for the Roosevelt administration, which promised to reshuffle the old cards of society. Among the numerous pieces of legislation passed in the early days of the Roosevelt administration, the one aimed at getting the economy back on its feet was the National Industrial Recovery Act (NIRA), which established the National Recovery Administration (NRA). Under the NIRA and the NRA, Roosevelt promised that millions of people would be back to work by the summer of 1933 and that their purchasing power would enable business to recover, since its products could once again be purchased.

Considering Williams's previously stated views on government relief of unemployment, his initial reaction to the NRA was that it was good as an emergency action only. Once the business "pump was primed," the NRA should be abandoned. In a cross-country trip of

8000 miles to assess America's reactions to the NRA, Williams reported that President Roosevelt was "popular" and that "business is better . . . but not much." Williams feared that success of the NRA would lead people to believe that government help was a long-run solution, much as it was believed to be in Great Britain and Europe. Williams recalled the postwar inflation in Germany as being caused by the printing of money by the government (that is, an expansion of the money supply beyond the bounds established by gold or silver reserve requirements), the same policy that Roosevelt was pursuing. Williams believed, then, that the NRA would create inflationary forces. Furthermore, he indicated that Americans were being led to believe that the federal government could solve all of their problems. Here, he reported, the lesson to be learned from Europe was that governments could only cut the bread "into smaller pieces," when what was needed was a larger loaf of bread. Although people were suspicious of business, and often blamed business for creating the depression, they failed to realize that only business could bake that bigger loaf; government could only redistribute what existed. For these reasons, the NRA should get business rolling, but then government should step aside.[12]

Explicit in Williams's opinion of the role of government vis-à-vis the worker was his idea that work is central to a person's self-esteem and community standing and that being "on the dole" or being compensated for not working, except as a temporary expedient, is bad for one's soul. Work had a spiritual significance and not working was degrading. One senses here that "idleness is the Devil's workshop," although Williams does not use that phrase, because the church, according to Williams, still believed that work was something dirty, the result of original sin. Rather than seeing workers as individuals, the church viewed them en masse as a broad social question, thus skimping on understanding the importance of work to individuals.[13] In brief, Williams concluded that neither the government nor the church understood the worker—the worker wanted work, which only business could create through new products and new markets, rather than relief from the state or homilies from the church.[14]

Germany and the USSR in 1933

Williams had visited the USSR in 1928 but had received a scare that kept him from returning there for some time. While talking with some coal miners, he was arrested, his passport was taken, and he was interrogated for three hours by the secret police before being released. After that visit, Williams was pessimistic about any economic progress the Soviets might make. Although they imported American and European machinery and engineers to tell them how to run the machinery, their industries would never succeed because their concept of how to manage was based on the idea of what was good for the Communist party and not what was good for the workers. Managers were selected because they were loyal to the party rather than because of their managerial or human skills.[15]

As the depression deepened in 1933, Williams wrote to his longtime friend Herbert Hoover, saying that he wanted a "first-hand view" of economic conditions in Poland, Germany, and the USSR.[16] In the USSR he saw how hard times were influencing international developments. The depression was worldwide and Williams sensed that the Germans and the Russians provided examples of how people turned to dictators in times of distress—the Russians had done so earlier, and now "Hitlerism" was on the rise in Germany.

In the USSR, Williams observed that the situation had worsened since his visit in 1928. Under Joseph Stalin, the collectivization of farmers, the institution of the five-year plan in 1927, and greater central economic planning had led to a decline in the economy. A great famine in the winter and spring of 1932–1933 had resulted in some 5 million deaths (according to Williams, the unofficial count was 10 million). The Americans, despite their own problems, were sending relief to Russia, just as they had done in the post–Russian revolution famine of 1921. Some 7 million USSR citizens were in prison, and workers were expected to work three days each week without pay for the government or they too would end up in Siberia. Williams toured Kiev, Kharkov, Dnieperostroy, and the Donetz Basin (all in the Ukraine) and his diary concluded that what the Soviets needed most of all was bread. In Kiev, he wrote, "the people are dirty and ill-fed"; yet between Kiev and Kharkov, wheat had been left in uncovered piles in the fields for lack of transport. In Kharkov, the factories were dirty and people showed little respect for their tools and their work. "There are no pickles, no potatoes . . . [and] boys are lying sick in the street—a naked baby too—with a big stomach from bad food, cabbage, and milk. . . . The chances seem poor that a big harvest [this year] will prevent awful conditions again this winter."[17]

What Williams had the misfortune to observe was partly famine but mostly the collectivization of peasant farmers, the *Kulaks*, by Joseph Stalin. Millions of *Kulaks* were liquidated by Stalin when they refused to join the collectives.[18] Williams saw nothing in the USSR to persuade him that the Russians and their satellites were doing any better in 1933 than they were in 1928.

In Germany, Williams got a close look at Adolf Hitler at a Nuremburg rally: "I was disappointed with Hitler's voice, magnetism, ideas. His Nuremburg speech was mostly platitudes about art, music, race-purity, and so on. . . . [Hitler's] advisers are mediocre if not positively pathological."[19]

Furthermore, he noted, "Goering, I think, is a well-known user of morphine, and another [Nazi] is a well-known lily who is now in charge of the youth movement."[20] Hitler's rise to power, according to Williams, came about because he promised jobs. This was, of course, not the first time Williams had concluded that workers listened to radicals when they were unemployed. In both Germany and Russia, Williams saw the dangers of turning to a strong central government for answers and warned that "government brings only hunger when it watches the golden eggs so closely that it discourages the goose from laying them. . . . [Americans] should not exact security while murdering opportunity."[21] In both Europe and America, Williams perceived the trend toward centralized economic planning as the solution for the ills of depressed nations. He did not like what he saw, and his experiences and observations confirmed his view that workers wanted opportunity, not security.

The Rise of the CIO

The 1930s bore witness to the first real successes at organizing workers on a national scale by industry rather than by craft. Attempts to organize workers regardless of their skills had met with only limited success previously—the National Labor Union of William Sylvis and the Noble Order of the Knights of Labor, led by Terence V. Powderly, had been colossal failures in the nineteenth century. The American Federation of Labor (AFL), a federation of craft workers formed in 1886, and numerous railroad brotherhoods, beginning as early as 1863, had demonstrated that unions could be successful when the workers held common skills. There had been some successful industrial unions, such as the garment workers, the milliners, and the mine workers, but their memberships were typically small vis-à-vis the craft workers. For example, almost 60 percent of the union members in 1929 were either in the building trades (919,000 members), predominantly AFL affiliates, or in transportation (892,000 members), mostly railroad brotherhoods. The largest noncraft unions were in mining (271,000 members) and garments and millinery (218,000 members).[22]

The political climate of the 1930s created the opportunity for industrial unionism to flourish. During the Hoover administration, the Federal Anti-Injunction Act of 1932, more commonly known as the Norris–La Guardia Act, was passed. This act, for all practical purposes, completely divested federal courts of injunctive powers in cases growing out of a labor dispute. In 1933, as mentioned earlier, Congress passed the National Industrial Recovery Act (NIRA). Section 7a of the NIRA, in similar but stronger language than that already existing in the Norris–La Guardia Act, specifically guaranteed that "employees shall have the right to organize and bargain collectively through representatives of their own choosing . . . free from interference, restraint, or coercion of employers."

When the NIRA was declared unconstitutional by the Supreme Court in 1935 (*United States vs. A.L.A. Schechter Poultry Corporation*), Congress quickly replaced it with a law that was even more pleasing to organized labor. The National Labor Relations Act, more commonly known as the Wagner Act, was far more definitive in what it expected of collective bargaining than was the NIRA. The Wagner Act guaranteed employees "the right to self-organization, to form, join, or assist labor organization, to bargain collectively through representatives of their own choosing, and to engage in concerted activities for the purpose of collective bargaining." In addition, it placed specific restrictions on what management could do by specifying five "unfair" management practices. To implement these provisions, the act established a National Labor Relations Board, which was granted the authority not only to issue cease-and-desist orders against employers violating the restrictions, but also to determine appropriate bargaining units and to conduct representation elections.[23]

After the passage of the Wagner Act, John L. Lewis, president of the United Mine Workers, led the fight for industrial unionism within the AFL. Rebuffed, Lewis formed the Committee for Industrial Organization (CIO—known after 1938 as the Congress of Industrial Organizations), whose purpose was to bring workers into unions regardless of occupation or skill level. The newly founded CIO enjoyed almost instant success and was able to claim almost 4 million members by 1937. With the legal climate created by the New Deal legislation, union membership spurted from 3.5 million at the turn of the decade to almost 9 million by 1939 (see Table 7.2). The price of this gain was an increase in the level of industrial strife.

TABLE 7.2.   Union Membership in the United States: 1930–1939

Year	Number of Union Members	Membership as Percent of Total Labor Force
1930	3,401,000	6.8
1931	3,310,000	6.5
1932	3,050,000	6.0
1933	2,689,000	5.2
1934	3,088,000	5.9
1935	3,584,000	6.7
1936	3,989,000	7.4
1937	7,001,000	12.0
1938	8,034,000	14.6
1939	8,763,000	15.8

Source: U.S. Bureau of the Census, *Historical Statistics*, pt. 1, p. 178. At the same time that the CIO was enjoying such tremendous success, the AFL was too—almost doubling its membership under the New Deal from 2,126,000 in 1933 to 4,000,000 in 1939. *See* Phillip Taft, *The AF of L from the Death of Gompers to the Merger* (New York: Harper and Row, 1957), p. 199.

Whiting Williams had a number of fascinating insights into industrial unionism—its causes, its techniques, and its likely outcomes. The insights that Williams had into the emerging CIO were possibly a result of his prior experiences with the AFL. Williams knew Samuel Gompers, John Frey, and other labor leaders, attended the AFL conventions occasionally, and had worked as a strikebreaker as well as a striker with the blessing of Gompers. Williams felt that America's labor leaders were levelheaded, responsible individuals who were sincere in their desire to protect the interests of the workers. They were not radicals who wished to overthrow the government, or even to form their own labor party, as Williams had seen happen in Europe and Great Britain. America's craft unions were conservative, "bread and butter" organizations that followed the advice of Richard Ely, one of the earliest students of the American labor movement, to "beware of demagoguery, especially political partyism . . . [and to] cast off the slavery of party politics."[24] Rather than forming a separate labor party, the American tradition had been for organized labor to work within the system and to confine its activities primarily to the economic domain of society. Craft unions, as Williams had observed, were job conscious. Since the job was crucial to the worker, Williams saw that unions were a normal part of the workers' desire to protect and enrich their situation. Cohesiveness was facilitated by craft unions because all workers within the union had a common job interest; thus skill levels were separated by crafts, reducing intraunion bickering and promoting common rules, which led to union solidarity.

The industrial union, however, was a different breed of cat. This type of unionism required a different source of power and control that focused not on the job, but on controlling the worker and the total employment situation. To gain power, unions needed members (the more the better) and dues (the more the better). The sheer number of workers would not suffice, however, unless the members felt a commonality of interests that bound their fate to that of their fellow unionists. Success came through a united front. The AFL had found its solidarity through the creation of a craft consciousness of mutual interests among boilermakers, carpenters, plumbers, and other craftsmen. Because the CIO had no such binding force, John L. Lewis needed to create an adversary relationship between labor and management that would say to the worker, "Join us for we can do something for you that management cannot." Instead of craft consciousness, the CIO needed a class consciousness that said, "It's us against them," the management. If skilled, semiskilled, and unskilled workers had no common job interests, allegedly they would have a common interest as the working class.

Williams had been critical of John L. Lewis before the formation of the CIO. As president of the United Mine Workers, Lewis had steadfastly chosen strikes and unemployment for his miners rather than bending to bad economic times and cooperating with management to make things better.[25] Williams felt that Lewis put his union's interests above the interests of the workers. As Lewis increased the militancy of the CIO to gain members, America entered a period of labor strife in the midst of a depression. The 1920s, a period of shop councils and union-management cooperation, were a time of peace compared with the turbulence of the latter half of the 1930s (see Tables 7.3 and 7.4). Whereas the disputes of the 1920s and early 1930s were primarily over wages and hours, in the last half of the 1930s strikes occurred mainly over union attempts to organize nonunion plants or to entrench their positions once a plant had been organized. In the steel, automobile, and rubber industries, violence and strikes erupted as the CIO tried to organize these large industries.

Williams interpreted the efforts of Lewis as political rather than economic. Lewis, Williams claimed, was serving the interests of the CIO rather than the worker. Williams also charged that Lewis's attempts to make the worker "class conscious" would lead to "class

TABLE 7.3. Work Stoppages and Their Causes: 1920–1929

		Causes				
		Wages and Hours		Union Organization		Other	
Year	Total	Number	Percent of total	Number	Percent of total	Number	Percent of total
1920	3411	2038	60	622	18	751	22
1921	2385	1501	63	373	16	511	21
1922	1112	583	52	208	19	321	29
1923	1553	721	46	308	20	524	34
1924	1249	537	43	244	20	468	37
1925	1301	537	41	219	17	545	42
1926	1035	478	46	206	20	351	34
1927	666	273	41	240	36	153	23
1928	620	222	36	226	36	172	28
1929	924	373	40	382	41	169	19

Source: U.S. Bureau of the Census, *Historical Statistics,* pt. 1, p. 179.

conflict – and chaos." Furthermore, Lewis was "too ruthless, auto-cratic, selfish and ambitious – politically and otherwise – to represent the typical, job-interested, middle-road worker."[26] By focusing on the differences between management and the worker, Lewis fomented conflict where there should be cooperation.

Williams also felt that the CIO organizers were typically the "least intelligent, the least reasonable, and the least honest" of all union members. Those who were attempting to organize the various plants were, in Williams's opinion, "promising their followers [prospective unionists] far and away too much."[27] Eager workers would join the union only to discover that either management could not

TABLE 7.4. Work Stoppages and Their Causes: 1930–1939

		Causes				
		Wages and Hours		Union Organization		Other	
Year	Total	Number	Percent of total	Number	Percent of total	Number	Percent of total
1930	651	284	44	207	32	160	24
1931	796	447	56	221	28	128	16
1932	852	560	66	162	19	130	15
1933	1672	926	55	533	32	213	13
1934	1817	717	39	835	46	265	15
1935	2003	760	38	945	47	298	15
1936	2156	756	35	1083	50	317	15
1937	4720	1410	30	2728	58	582	12
1938	2772	776	28	1385	50	611	22
1939	2639	699	26	1411	54	529	20

Source: U.S. Bureau of the Census, *Historical Statistics,* pt. 1, p. 179. Another useful source on labor strife during the New Deal is Irving Bernstein, *Turbulent Years: A History of the American Worker, 1933–1941* (Boston: Houghton-Mifflin, 1969).

afford their demands or that the union could not deliver on its promises, or both. The result was disgruntled workers who embarked on a series of "sit-down" strikes on an unprecedented level. These strikes were illegal in the sense that a contract between labor and management had been signed, but some workers refused to work under the agreement and prevented others from working, too. In Akron, Ohio, for example, 10,000 workers at the Goodrich Tire and Rubber factory were out of work for a week because 15 dissidents staged a sit-down strike. This minority tyrannized the majority, repudiated its union leaders, and violated its contractual agreement. Williams observed that this was a result of the inexperience and ineptitude of the CIO leaders since the craft unions would not have condoned unofficial strikes and would have had greater control over their members.[28] Indeed, the common practice among the craft unions was to levy fines on their own members if they engaged in "wildcat," or unauthorized, work stoppages. One measure of a union's effectiveness was its ability to keep its members in line.

Union security vis-à-vis management was another matter. One measure of a union's bargaining strength was the agreements it could convince management to make regarding who would be hired and who would collect the union dues. The CIO sought a "closed shop," that is, its goal was to obtain agreement by management that a person must be a union member before he or she would be hired. A second goal was the "check-off" of dues. Under this system each worker signed a form that permitted the employer to deduct the union dues from his or her salary. The employer then turned the dues over to the union. If these goals could be met, the union would be assured that no one worked unless he or she was a union member, and the onus of collecting dues would be shifted to management. Williams saw this as a power play, because "it is a great question whether any CIO-type union can hold skilled, semi-skilled, and unskilled workers together without the help of the closed shop and the check-off."[29] The power base for the union, then, rested in controlling who got jobs and in requiring the payment of dues. There would be no "free-riders." This power base was quite different, in Williams's view, from that of the AFL craft situation, which focused on the concern of the worker over the job; rather, the CIO position emphasized union security over worker and job security. Thus, Lewis and his CIO cohorts were politically rather than economically motivated. The establishment and preservation of the union came first.

Once recognized as the legitimate bargaining agent, the union needed to control job access (through the closed shop) and to maintain an income of dues (through the check-off). Furthermore, according to Williams, the union leaders had to keep telling the workers that without the union they would be taken advantage of by management. This constant "we" versus "them" meant that union leaders needed "to keep stirring up disputes, disturbances and stoppages [in order to] justify further dues."[30] Under these circumstances, the union and the employer would be constantly struggling for the loyalty of the worker. This was an anathema to Whiting Williams who saw the need for better leaders, improved communications, and an understanding that emphasized the mutual interests of workers and managers.

Among those who also held Williams's view about the CIO was the famous labor economist, John R. Commons. A staunch proponent of organized labor and a longtime friend of the late Samuel Gompers, Commons felt that the CIO would fail because it did not conform to the innate conservatism of the American labor movement.[31] Many Americans felt that the CIO was Communist-inspired, and Whiting Williams was fundamentally of that opinion as well. Williams attended a labor-management relations conference at Stanford University in 1939 where he heard Harry Bridges, organizer of the West Coast longshoremen, speak. Bridges said, "Hate your boss — love your union!" He also advocated dismembering the AFL, breaking contracts if doing so would further organized labor's goals, and forming a labor party.[32] Williams felt that Bridges served the Communist cause (even though Bridges himself denied that he was a Communist), as did the "left-leaners" in the auto workers union.

Williams felt that poor management practices fostered the conditions under which agitators could make progress. The agitators did not cause the problems but fed on workers' emotions "only when the management has gotten out of touch with its individual workers." The idea of a "working class struggle" was a meaningless phrase used to arouse and further antagonism for political purposes: "The worker is not interested in economic philosophy. He wants fair hours and living wages and he tries to obtain these in a reasonable manner."[33] Cures for labor problems did not lie in grand schemes or in revolution but in the simple need to "keep closer contact than ever before with one another in the office, the warehouse, and the plant." By focusing on human relationships, especially at the level of contact between the first-line supervisor and the worker, and by listening and being responsive to valid grievances, the workers' interest in the agitators would be kept to a minimum.

As supporting evidence, Williams told of the Saar Valley coal mines where the workers were German but the supervisors were French. Just a few years before, these two nations had faced each other from the trenches; now one was management and the other was labor. Yet the result was remarkably successful — why? Williams found that the French supervisors spent "the first two hours of each working day below ground talking with miners about ventilation, equipment, safety," and other work and worker-related subjects. The Germans were surprised at this practice for it had been their experience with German supervisors that a manager never talked to a worker unless something went wrong! This created hostility and apprehension, because the only communication between the worker and the supervisor occurred under unpleasant circumstances. With the French supervisors, however, the communications were regular and pleasant. This type of labor-management communications was advocated by Williams (recall that he also had praised Western Electric's practice of button talks, which involved upper-level management getting out from behind its desk to talk with the workers).[34]

Why was Williams so alarmed and anti-CIO? Because he saw these union leaders as political, not economic, in motivation; because they fomented class consciousness and divisiveness rather than the mutuality of interests between labor and management; because they were more concerned with the union's continuance as an organization than with the worker's well-being; and because they needed to maintain an adversary relationship in order to sustain their existence. Williams saw the AFL type of union as responsible, economically focused, and in tune with the workers' needs. Whereas Williams would accept the AFL, he saw the CIO as a troublemaker. The solution to the problems of an industrial civilization did not lie in further conflict, but in cooperation; not in divisiveness, but in listening with sensitivity; not in ignoring, but in keeping in touch with people at the working level; and not by isolating "we versus them," but in opening up our understanding of how all of us are so much alike in our fundamental humanness.

Tragic Times for the Family

In 1922, Whiting Williams had moved his family into a sturdy two-story house in Cleveland Heights, a fashionable suburb of Cleveland. The 1920s were especially busy years for Williams, and he traveled a great deal in his newfound double life as the white collar hobo. He sometimes embarrassed his wife, Caroline, who had to pick up this unkempt character at the train station and then transport him into the finer parts of Cleveland.[35] Caroline Williams was active in community and church organizations and performed as a violinist in the Cleveland Symphony for many years. Carol, the daughter, attended the Hathaway-Brown School and inherited the family's musical talents. She graduated Phi Beta Kappa from Smith College in 1929, and the future held great promise for her as a pianist. She studied music at the Sorbonne in Paris for one year and was a young woman of exceptional talent with a fine, attractive face of great sensitivity. Tragedy would end this young lady's life in 1932 at the age of twenty-five. She had been on a date with Julian W. Feiss, the son of a neighbor. Upon their return to the Feiss home, they smelled gas in the garage. Julian lit a match, and both were badly burned in the explosion. Carol died in the hospital, August 20, 1932, of an embolism caused by the burns. In her memory, the family established the Carol Williams Memorial Scholarship Fund at the Cleveland Institute of Music. When Whiting's father, Benjamin J. Williams, died in 1933 at the age of ninety-one, Beatty and Whiting established a trust fund in the name of their father and their mother (who had died in 1910) at the Shelby (Ohio) Public Library.

Shortly after Carol's death, Williams began his long years of correspondence with the philosopher Ernest Hocking. This relationship will be explored in Chapter 8, but the timing of its beginning appears to have been connected with Williams's search for some answers that life had not provided. During this search for philosophy and the broader meaning of life following the death of Carol, tragedy was to strike Williams again. The health of his wife, Caroline, began to deteriorate, and the diagnosis was cancer of the spine. Her death on July 2, 1938, left yet another gap in Williams's life.

Changing Times

The American Great Depression, which began in 1929, was an economic, social, political, and psychological watershed. Whiting Williams, born in the nineteenth century in a middle western American community, was imbued with the Protestant ethic that work was crucial to a person's well-being. The job was a central part of one's life, the measuring rod for oneself, one's family, and one's standing in the community. America was changing, however, as the depression brought new interpretations of the role of government in economics and in schemes to establish social floors and hedges against social maladies, such as unemployment. No longer would the virtues of self-help, thrift, and hard work be seen as the keys to success. If you were down, the government helped you up; if you lost your savings or bank account, the government reimbursed you; if you had saved nothing for retirement, the government would provide a pension, and so on through a host of social measures designed to take some of the sting out of life.

Whiting Williams lived long enough to see American values change from an emphasis on opportunity to one on security. All through the 1920s Williams had seen this psychology of scarcity operating in Great Britain and Europe and warned that schemes such as unemployment insurance would never work in America. His misfortune was in living long enough to see these very things happen. America did become more security conscious, and Williams could never accept this. As Williams's friend, former President Herbert Hoover wrote to Williams: "You examine our breed of tramps again. They are changing. . . . I'll furnish the overalls."[36] The new breed of tramps no longer even pretended to look for work, relying, instead, upon others to provide it for them. These were indeed the dark years, and Williams would have more to say about the trends he saw.

EIGHT

Still More Miles to Go

Family, Friends, and Philosophers

Although the 1930s had brought family tragedies, some other events had helped to lighten the load a little. One of these occurrences, which was amusing at first but became embarrassing later, was the appearance of an "imposter." Williams had acquired a national reputation as one who traveled in the guise of a worker but who really was a person of refinement and education. Beginning in 1933, an individual began to represent himself as Whiting Williams, but claiming that he was temporarily without funds and needed financial help in order to continue his research on the worker. This person would request room and board for an evening (free, of course), ask that someone cash his check (no account, naturally), or borrow a car (which was never returned). The imposter was described as a "piano playing, well educated man who wore horn-rimmed glasses and was a heavy drinker."[1] Of course, all those who had been victimized traced the real Whiting Williams, whose replies included an apology, an explanation, a photograph of himself to prove that he was not the culprit, and a brief history of how this imposter had operated before. The imposter finally stopped his charade in 1935 but was never apprehended.

Another imitator of Whiting Williams was far more honest about what he was doing. Robert Jorgensen, son of Headmaster Arthur Jorgensen of Groton Academy in Massachusetts, had read of Williams's experiences and wanted to duplicate the feat. He spent three months "on the road" living the double life in 1951. His letters to Williams indicated that the job was "still crucial" but that it was much more difficult to be a hobo in the 1950s than it must have been in the 1920s. Williams sent frequent encouragement, but young Jorgensen gave up his travels to take a supervisor's job in a paper factory in St. Louis. He later thanked Williams for his inspiration and said he felt that he was a better supervisor because of his experiences. To this, Williams replied that "[the experiences] you got were better for handling people problems than a college education — you can't learn that [handling personnel problems] from books."[2]

Williams's son, Harter Whiting Williams, also got some first-hand experience interviewing workers and union officials in conjunction with some consulting work that his father was doing. Harter, a 1936 graduate of Western Reserve University, would establish his own career later as a consultant in transportation with his headquarters in Washington, D.C.[3]

Whiting Williams gained a new partner in life on August 4, 1941, when he married Dorothy Rogers. Dorothy and Whiting had known each other since 1923 when Dorothy had been a private nurse for Whiting's sister, Florence. Dorothy later moved to Chicago, Illinois, where she became chief administrator of the nursing program at Presbyterian Hospital. At the time of their marriage in Oak Park, Illinois, Dorothy was forty-five and Whiting was sixty-three years old. Dorothy called it a "marriage of congeniality" that grew into a good marriage of shared travels, common interests in the Cleveland Symphony, and great-grandchildren (provided by Harter's daughters). Dorothy recalled that Whiting was always interested in what others had on their minds and even used their honeymoon to talk to the workers.

Through the years, Williams had made the acquaintance of numerous important people. Through his officer's position in the Oberlin Alumni Association he knew Katherine Wright, another Oberlin alumna and sister to the Wright brothers, Orville and Wilbur. Neither Orville nor Wilbur had attended Oberlin, but Williams encouraged them to be active in the alumni group since each had received an honorary doctorate from Oberlin.

The story is told that after one Oberlin alumni affair Whiting's wife, Caroline, said, "What a seedy-looking lot the Oberlin alumni are — who was the man in the baggy brown suit that had never been pressed?" Whiting's reply: "That was Orville Wright."[4]

Williams's most prized friendship was the one with Herbert C. Hoover. Hoover had read *What's On The Worker's Mind?* the book that made Whiting Williams a national figure, and had commented on its value in encouraging shop councils as a means to let workers air their grievances and become involved in their work situations. As

Hoover's career progressed from secretary of commerce to the thirty-first president of the United States, and for years afterward, they exchanged greetings and news annually. One of Hoover's epistles was framed and placed on the wall in Williams's office; it read, "With your mind and instinct you cannot go wrong on anything."[5] Later, Hoover would write, "It is a blessing to the world that you still live in it"; and Williams replied, "All your fellow humans are delighted to see you approaching your ninetieth [birthday]—and wishing you many more."[6] Hoover would see his ninetieth birthday, but no more, thus ending these exchanges of mutual admiration that had taken place for over forty years.

When the Cleveland Federation for Charity and Philanthropy celebrated its fiftieth anniversary in 1963, its honored speaker was its first executive director, Whiting Williams. Williams received a "spontaneous standing ovation" from the business and civic leaders as he received the Distinguished Service Award of the Cleveland federation. He spoke on "How Federated Giving—and Planning—Came About," a speech that traced the pioneering efforts of the Cleveland community in "coordinated benevolence," which had brought national recognition to Cleveland.[7] Williams was also honored with a doctor of laws degree from Fenn College (predecessor to Cleveland State University) in 1957. Then in 1968, Cleveland State University awarded him another honorary doctorate of laws.

Accolades from others who had been influenced by Williams included a letter from Professor Morris S. Viteles, a prominent industrial psychologist at the University of Pennyslvania, who wrote: "Your pioneering work has been much neglected by the savants."[8] Tom Spates, erstwhile vice-president of industrial relations at the General Foods Corporation and later a professor at Yale University, wrote that he was writing a book and that he would list Williams as a "pioneer" in the quest for better human understanding in industry.[9] Over the years Williams had prided himself on his relationships with leaders of labor such as John Frey, Matthew Woll, William Murray, and Samuel Gompers. These stalwarts were dead, but Williams continued to praise labor leaders who sought to build bridges between labor and management. His favorite was Clinton S. Golden, a founder and vice-president of the United Steelworkers of America, who was noted for his attempts to secure industrial democracy in the workplace.[10] After his retirement, Golden lectured at Harvard University, consulted, and told Williams that he felt that labor and management had made a lot of progress since the "old days."[11]

Williams was also interested in building bridges across disciplines, particularly through his goal of turning his experiences and observations into a philosophy. Although Williams did not begin his long correspondence with philosopher William Ernest Hocking until shortly after the death of his daughter, Carol, in 1932, Williams's interest in philosophy actually began at Oberlin, was furthered by his seminary year at the University of Chicago, and continued when he joined the Philosophical Club of Cleveland in 1918. The members of this club were Cleveland community leaders who met on a regular basis to discuss philosophical, social, and/or municipal problems. Meredith B. Colket, now director emeritus of the Western Reserve Historical Society, spent many years in this philosophers' club with Whiting Williams. He recalled that Williams was as active in the club as he could be, considering his frequent travels. He also remembered that Williams often told his fellow members that the workings of their brains would improve if they gave themselves a brisk scalp massage each morning to "stimulate their thinking."[12]

Williams's long years of correspondence with Hocking indicated his desire to crystallize his experiences into a philosophy. Hocking was a native of Cleveland who had moved through academia to become the Alford Professor of Philosophy at Harvard University. He was a devotee of the psychologist-philosopher William James, and it was James's pragmatism that led Hocking to emphasize the importance of experience in shaping philosophy.[13] On this common ground of experience, Williams and Hocking found their rapport. Hocking encouraged Williams to develop his philosophy, because he felt that all of us were victims of "occupational remoteness" in the sense that we really knew very little about the work of others and that Williams's experiences as a worker would help to close the gap. Hocking liked Williams's "shirt sleeve empiricism" because he considered himself an "empirical idealist—one who founds his faiths on experience."[14] As Williams began working on the manuscript that became *America's Mainspring*, he received support from Hocking, who also feared the path chosen by America:

> I am feeling depressed and rebellious over our americanism [*sic*], both its complacent side and its disturbed side. Complacent in its soft education, ducking the hard disciplines from the primer grade upward; its vapid passivity toward insanity in the arts; and in a stumbling foreign policy in which Brother [John Foster] Dulles mistakes brittleness for firmness and strength.[15]

Williams agreed, for he would later write of the decline of individual responsibility and the trend toward collectivism in American life. "[I am] more and more convinced that our fundamental 'wish for worth' is a better explanation for human nature than Marx's materialism."[16] Hocking and Williams continued to correspond with each other until the autumn of 1965, when Hocking's illness and his death in 1966 removed one more of Williams's cohorts.

Williams also had some correspondence with the noted theologian, Reinhold Niebuhr, on the meaning of work. Niebuhr emphasized that only work done for the love of God was worthwhile, while Williams disagreed, arguing that "self-satisfaction" and "pride in possession" were legitimate rewards of labor.[17] After a few exchanges of articles for the other to read, Williams and Niebuhr concluded their correspondence.

Parapsychology, particularly extrasensory perception (ESP), was also one of Williams's interests. As a child he had been fascinated by the psychic powers of his sister, Florence, who had been tested and retested by professionals, consistently displaying her extrasensory powers. As a man, Williams was curious again about how ESP worked and whether or not it could be used to improve human communications and understanding. J. B. Rhine, of Duke University, had formed a Foundation for Research on the Nature of Man, and Williams subscribed to the foundation's publications and contributed money to its research efforts as early as 1954. Over the years, Williams noted that there was little research being done that was leading to positive results. "I've never been much interested in the matter of life after death," he wrote to Rhine, but in "mind over matter through telepathy" to improve human communication. All of the foundation's work had yielded little, Williams felt. One of Rhine's associates defended the foundation and chided Williams for not reading all of the reports. For example, one researcher had found "that the electrical energy of plants can be influenced by an experimenter."[18] This did not impress Williams, who responded that he had been "forced to feel that I had shown very bad judgment in aiding an enterprise so manifestly unable to secure financial support from any great number of intelligent persons."[19] With that, Williams tendered his resignation from the foundation.

Williams remained active far past the normal retirement age of most people. He continued his travels, worked on *America's Mainspring* sporadically, corresponded with philosophers and friends, and did not vacate his office on Euclid Avenue in Cleveland until 1968, when he reached the age of ninety. He believed what he wrote about the role of work in a person's life.

The Work Simplification Conferences

In 1932, Allan H. Mogensen began a program to train managers and other employees in motion economy and work simplification. Mogensen, a 1924 graduate of Cornell University who had taught engineering at the University of Rochester, was greatly influenced by the scientific management pioneer, Frank B. Gilbreth. Frank Gilbreth and his wife, Lillian, had indicated the economies to be achieved by a thorough study of workers' motions. The Gilbreths advocated worker involvement in making improvements in the job and emphasized the need for training people in the "one best way" to do work.[20] Mogensen continued in the Gilbreth tradition by emphasizing the importance of creativity in looking for improvements as well as in obtaining the full cooperation of top management, supervisors, and the workers. The idea was to get people to "work smarter, not harder," by tapping the ideas of those who were closely involved in the actual operations.[21]

Mogensen was familiar with Williams's writings concerning the worker and the proper relationship between labor and management. In 1939, Mogensen invited Williams to participate in the annual conference on work simplification held at Lake Placid, New York. In 1950, a winter conference was added at Sea Island, Georgia, and Williams was a regular participant in these conferences from 1939 until 1964. The format was for Williams to present his experiences and philosophy to those in attendance, followed by a question and answer period. In 1960, 1961, and 1962, Mogensen taped Williams's segment of the program, revealing a portion of history that would have otherwise been lost.[22] The tapes reveal Williams as a master storyteller and a superb mimic of the dialects and jargon of the workers he had encountered over more than half a century of travels.

According to Mogensen, "Whiting Williams had a great deal to do with my being certain that I was on the right track in following my belief which I arrived at in 1930—that the person doing the job knows more about that job than anyone else and therefore is the one person best fitted to improve it."[23] To date, several thousand people from nearly 800 companies have participated in the work simplification conferences and for twenty-five years they heard the experiences of the white collar hobo. These experiences, told in Williams's unique anecdotal style, emphasized the need for managers to pay attention to their employees, to communicate, to listen, to provide opportunities for hope and pride in life and work.

And Miles To Go

Williams was an indefatigable traveler. In 1956, at the age of seventy-eight, he made his sixteenth trip to Europe and his third tour of the USSR; at the age of seventy-nine, he toured Australia and New Zealand; and in 1962, at the age of eighty-four, he went around the world from America to Japan, Taiwan, Hong Kong, Bangkok, Calcutta, Bombay, Cairo, and back home. His concerns in these later travels were the broader social and economic issues that faced the nations of the world. His premise was that one could judge the different "isms" of the world — communism, socialism, and Americanism — by how closely they fitted the "nature of man, what we human beings amount to." These different "isms" were "based on different theories of human nature, human values, human goals, human incentives; what it is that we humans stand most willing to work for, live for, and, if necessary, to die for."[24]

Since Williams had first traveled to Great Britain in 1920, France and Germany in 1921, and Russia in 1928, he could trace the development of these countries over a long period of time. In Russia, for instance, he found that the situation had worsened over the years, even though he did not see starving peasants in the Ukraine, as he had during his 1933 trip when Stalin was trying to force collectivization of the farms. Despite some improvements in feeding people, Williams concluded that communism had not created "the absolutely indispensable will to work." Part of the problem was caused by the absolute power of the rulers of the USSR. To illustrate, Williams told the story of the man who had been imprisoned for shouting "Down with Stalin!" After four years, he was released, but did not know that in the meantime, the government had decided to downgrade Stalin's accomplishments. The recently released man was so happy and repentant that he shouted, "Long live Stalin!" Whereupon he was returned to the same cell! There was also the story of the citizen who said that

Krushchev did not have enough brains to rule the country—whereupon the citizen "was given ten years for being disloyal plus twenty years for divulging a state secret!" "To whom do you complain?" Williams asked a Soviet worker. The manager? ("no, because they are selected by the Communist Party"); the government? ("no, because they too are Party members"); the party? ("no, because communism is the ideal system and only crazy people have complaints").[25] In short, the worker had no outlet for grievances.

Socialism in Great Britain and France had also failed to deliver its promises. In Great Britain, a high-ranking member of the Labour party told Williams "that the working man has let us [Great Britain] down." Williams disagreed: it was not the working man who had failed, but the system, which "gave no reward and threatened no punishment . . . [because] nobody stands to gain by effort and nobody stands to lose by lack of it."[26] It was a system that asked "everybody to tighten his belt, but persuaded nobody to roll up his sleeves." In Great Britain, the question "Who is Bill Smith?" meant "What is his social class?" not "What does he count in making the whole thing move?"

Both communism and socialism were predicated on the idea that we "renounce our freedom and give all responsibility and control to an all-powerful government which promises to cover our backs, fill our bellies, and satisfy our purely physical needs." Both of these "isms" assumed that people did not want challenge, but preferred to be taken care of. In Williams's view, this was not what people really wanted, nor did these "isms" conform to the basic nature of people. These "isms" had to be sustained by fear, not by hope; by comfort, not by challenge; by security, not by opportunity.

The third "ism," Americanism, conformed more closely to human nature because it "prompts us to compete with each other for the opportunity to earn not simply money but also self-respect and honor by improving our usefulness" to others. The danger that Williams saw in 1957 was that America was getting more and more like Great Britain in a dangerous trend toward a welfare state:

> The greatest threat on the American scene today is the way we are all trying to get more subsidies from the government in exchange for the increased power we give to [the government]. Every day we are urged to pay less honor to the producers of useful goods and services and more honor to political officials who try to win votes . . . by distributing physical comforts not according to usefulness and merit, but according to *need*.[27]

What was the source of this threat? Williams told an Australian audience that he was alarmed

> as I go about the world in seeing that today we seem to have been losing faith in the possibilities of human nature, particularly the possibilities of the individual. . . . [That is] a moral retreat away from the possibilities and the responsibilities of the individual and seeking refuge in the mass and the collective.[28]

America was moving toward socialism because our elections were "auctions," with each party trying to outbid the other to get votes.[29] Our survival depended upon our "will to work," to produce an abundance rather than to share less and less. As he had noted earlier, governments typically focused on slicing the bread into smaller pieces when what was needed was a larger loaf. To counter the trend, Williams advised that each of us should follow the advice of Evan Pugh, a Welsh coal miner. Pugh and Williams had worked together in a mine in Rhondda Valley, Wales, some one thousand feet down and two miles away from the entrance. One day Williams had asked Pugh what to do if he should lose his sense of direction. Pugh replied:

> 'Tis easy lad. All y'needs t'do is always keep a'walkin' with the air a-blowin' in your face, and by that you will come to safety and salvation. Y'see the great fans up the top push down a great volume of air to take away the gases raised free by our picks at the face of the seam. Walk against that draft and you'll walk to the hoist in safety.[30]

It was not the direction of least resistance that led to safety, but the path that ran counter to the ongoing flow that held promise. Leadership consisted of offering challenges and attendant risks:

> [People] do not, in the long run, follow the line of least resistance; we have no respect for the leaders who ask so little of us that when we give it we can't think any better of ourselves than before we were asked . . . but we will go through hell for the leader who asks almost the impossible of us, provided that when we give it he shares with us the right to think better of ourselves.[31]

In other words, was it not more reasonable to assume that people desired challenge—enough to stretch their abilities but not so much as to frustrate them? Without challenge, without clear goals, obviously there would be a great deal of slack between our abilities and our tasks, leaving each of us with the void of being a cipher, of little or no use to ourselves or to others.

America's Mainspring and the Great Society

In the mid-1950s Williams began to conceive another book. The intent was to "express his disquiet" over trends in American society; specifically, the decline of individualism and the rise of collectivism in American life. Williams feared what collectivism would do to American society. From his experiences and observations, he identified nine developments that he believed would occur if the trend toward more centralized government prevailed:

I. More recognition and honor will go to our elected [officials] as the distributors of gifts and less to the producers of needed goods and services. As rapidly as this attracts a lower caliber of enterpriser and industrialist, the more he will serve as a scape-goat and the more difficult will become the kind of teamwork between government and business required for making prayer-answering jobs abundant everywhere.

II. Leaders dependent on votes naturally prefer to deal less with individuals than with organized and manageable groups, whether of farmers, wage-earners, the sick, the elderly or whatever. This is certain to telescope our world-famous job-ladder of opportunity in exchange for an easier, surer job-platform.

III. Unless wisely handled, huge sums in relief, family supplements, group subsidies, price supports, occupational and area developments, etc., discourage industrial productivity. When these "free" gifts are seen to depend less on merit than on need, then dependence and demoralization spread.

IV. A well-filled federal treasury tends to create a one-party government.

V. For whatever benevolent or other purpose levied, a Welfare State's taxes tend to become "cannibalistic" — to consume its tax-payers.

VI. From time beyond memory, Governments have been tempted to solve their money problems and "increase prosperity" by the hidden, cruelest, most dishonest and demoralizing form of taxation — Inflation.

VII. When welfare governments expand their services, they find it constantly harder to furnish the know how, the efficiency and especially the evenhanded fairness, required to avoid wide-spread irritation and the loss of public respect.

VIII. For preserving its sovereignty against "dangerous" criticism, every government is tempted, especially in time of crisis, to expand its control over public communications and opinion.

IX. As centralized political authority increases, it is tempted to displace the traditional Code of Respectability and Honor

> with the government's "Morality." . . . No human posses-
> sor of excessive, unshared, unbalanced and appealless
> power, whether individual, institution or government, can
> be trusted never to abuse it.[32]

One needs only a basic understanding of American and world history to evaluate Williams's predictions, which were printed in 1967. First, our political leaders are far more recognizable by the public than are our business leaders, with but few exceptions; and business leaders are often held responsible for economic decline, oil gluts, high prices, and other societal blights. Second, the power of well-organized interest groups that lobby for special purposes is quite evident, as is the emergence, in the past decade, of class-action lawsuits. Third, although difficult to prove that dependence and demoralization have spread with increasing public expenditure for social programs, certainly there has been a dramatic decline in industrial productivity, which has shifted America's position from that of a world industrial leader to a follower. Fourth, while we have not attained a one-party government, there is a familial resemblance between our two political parties. Fifth, no comment should be necessary about the increase in taxes that has accompanied increased welfare programs. Sixth, again no elucidation is necessary about the rate of inflation since 1967. Regarding Williams's seventh prediction, people still expect efficiency in government; and we have been able to protect the rights he worried about in his eighth. Who wishes to recall, however, the political turmoil of a presidency that would stoop to dishonesty and trickery to win another election, as Williams's ninth prediction foresaw? In retrospect, Williams's perception of the trends that would accompany the growth of big government and the welfare state were remarkably accurate.

America's Mainspring was not, by any measure, Williams's best book. Most of the material came from prior publications, speeches, or from his presentations at the work simplification conferences. Only in the last chapter did he begin to show what his years of travel, interviews, observations, and study had produced—the ability to look at our society and its values from both a longitudinal and a cross-cultural perspective. His evaluation of the "Great Society," for example, was not Republican-inspired Presbyterianism, but a summary of what he had seen developing in Europe, Great Britain, and the USSR over the past half of a century. He applied his analysis of those developments to what he witnessed in America and produced a remarkable portrait of our societal trends. Similarly, he took his experiences as a worker and foresaw the role of unions; the need for first-line supervisors to be responsive to their workers; the central value of work in people's lives; and the universal mainspring of the wish for worth and the confirmation of that worth gained through the acceptance, recognition, esteem, and honor of others.

Our white collar hobo used his remarkable skills as a participant-observer of work and life to add something to all of our lives. Whiting Williams ceased his earthly travels April 14, 1975, at the age of ninety-seven years, one month, and three days, thus ending the odyssey of the white collar hobo.

Epilogue

Whiting Williams merits study because he broke new ground in understanding work, workers, and their relationship to management and to society. In *The Story of Mankind*, H. W. Van Loon stated that "the history of the world is the record of man in quest of his daily bread and butter." Williams added to this record during a period when American labor-management relations stood at a crossroads. After World War I, in the midst of industrial unrest and strife, America could have gone the way of Europe—socialism, separate labor parties, increased radicalization of labor, and a greater cleavage between the working class and the rest of society. Instead, America turned to union-management cooperation, shop councils for employee representation, "bread and butter" unions, increased educational opportunities to provide social ladders, and improved human relations on the job. Times would change later, but neither American economic development nor American labor-management relations have ever reached the collectivist extremes that can be observed abroad.

The research of Whiting Williams touched on numerous areas that today might be classified as personnel management, industrial or organizational sociology, human relations, and labor-management relations. In Williams's day, these areas were either just emerging or yet to become manifest. An evaluation of Williams's contributions must be made in the light of his times, although it is possible to corroborate his conclusions with the findings of modern researchers. In general, two broad statements can be made about Williams's contributions to our understanding of modern labor-management relations: (1) his research method as a "participant-observer" was unique and systematic;

and (2) the results of his research were advanced for his times and antedate some modern research findings.

A number of historians have suggested that past research has placed too much emphasis on the synonymity of the history of labor-management relations with the history of the union as an institution. Auerbach, for example, has indicated that most of the histories have been institutional because better records are available for such studies and, as a result, "American workers have been long invisible men."[33] Field research began with Frederic LePlay (1806–1882), a nineteenth-century researcher of how workers lived. Although he was more of an observer than a participant, he visited nearly every country in Europe, occasionally lodged for brief periods with workers' families, and studied how they budgeted their money and raised their children and how their families functioned as social units. While LePlay did not work alongside his subjects, his observational research method was considered pioneering. He was one of the first to study working life firsthand rather than to speculate about it. Two nineteenth-century participant-observers, Paul Goehre and Walter Wyckoff, were discussed in Chapter 1. Although both published their experiences in the 1890s, neither of them followed up on their travels with other research.

The phrase "participant-observer" was coined in 1924 by Eduard Lindeman to describe the role of an observer planted inside a group to corroborate the findings of an outside observer.[34] Eventually, this research technique changed from one involving a "plant" to one involving an outsider who was accepted by the group as one of its own.[35] For those who study labor-management relations, there are basically three research methods: (1) the survey questionnaire; (2) the interview; and (3) participation-observation. Robert Dubin, a renowned sociologist, has said that of these methods, the participant-observer method is far superior for studying work.[36] With this method, it is far easier to obtain a person's real feelings and to develop empathy for what the situation involves. Despite the value of this research method, the difficulties are obvious: how to find the time to become a member of the group being studied; how to move freely about the workplace to make more contacts and to gather more than limited information; how to avoid being "discovered," and so on. These difficulties undoubtedly explain the relatively limited use of this research technique. It was through this most difficult but most efficacious research method, however, that Whiting Williams performed his inquiries, making him the first authentic participant-observer of labor-management relations in the twentieth century. Through his systematic use of this research technique, he was able to gather firsthand insights into what was happening in industry.

The contributions that mark Whiting Williams as a perceptive social scientist who pioneered our understanding of the relations between labor and management can be summarized as: (1) the identification of the importance of work to a person's economic and social well-being; (2) the fact that job status exerts an influence on defining a person's standing in the community; (3) the existence of a job hierarchy within the workplace; (4) the knowledge that the workplace is part of a larger social system; (5) the revelation that wages are used to make social comparisons rather than being perceived solely for their absolute value; (6) the theory that people are motivated by a wish for worth rather than by instincts; (7) the observation that as wages rise, workers substitute leisure for work; (8) the theory that unions originate from needs for security and job consciousness; (9) the reminder that the first-line supervisor is crucial to sound labor-management relations and needs to develop an understanding of the "human angle"; (10) the belief that unemployment has a spiritual impact as well as an economic and social one; and (11) the observation that labor-management relations in various countries are influenced by the educational and other opportunities presented, and thus, that America provided a job ladder and hope rather than developing a working class consciousness as other countries had done.

These findings certainly indicate Williams's role as a pioneer, yet for some reason his contributions are rarely mentioned by modern scholars. It is, for example, common practice to refer to Ruth Cavan and Katherine Ranck's *The Family and the Depression* and Mirra Komarovsky's *The Unemployed Man and His Family* as the pioneering studies of unemployment. Williams's experiences and insights from the 1920s and 1930s, two decades ahead of the alleged pioneers, are seldom mentioned, yet their findings were remarkably similar to his.[37] Williams, who felt that management and labor could have mutual goals and did not need to be enemies, as some have insisted, would have appreciated some of the fairly recent findings of Theodore Purcell. Purcell found that even though workers were prounion, this did not make them antimanagement. Rather, the workers had a "dual allegiance," one to the company and one to the union, and "did not feel that their allegiance [to one or the other] was like a cake . . . so that one side's gain would mean the other side's loss."[38]

Williams had proposed many years earlier that the union was not a "bad guy" and that labor and management could work together.

Later participant-observers corroborated Williams's findings, providing an audit of his perceptiveness. One example was Hyacinthe Dubreuil, a Frenchman who considered himself a "moderate socialist" and came to America in 1927 to see if the more radical elements of the French labor movement were correct in their conclusion that Taylorism exploited labor. After fifteen months as a worker in American factories, including a stint on the Ford Motor Company assembly line, he went back to France as a believer in scientific management and Taylorism. As Williams had observed, but from another perspective, Dubreuil marveled at the wages and amenities that the American workers enjoyed. Would an American go to France to live and work? Never! But would a Frenchman come to American to live and work? Yes! He also found that the factory managers placed less emphasis on the hierarchy of authority and that there was little if any class consciousness in America.[39]

Stanley Mathewson worked as a laborer, machine operator, and conveyor assembler in nonunionized factories to see if the restriction of output was exclusively a union phenomenon. His conclusion — no; this practice was widespread among all workers. Furthermore, workers were not "speeded" by management, as was often alleged, but were typically underworked.[40] Another student of the practice of output restriction was Donald Roy, who spent eleven months as a radial drill operator in a machine shop. He distinguished between "daywork goldbricking" (that is, pure and simple loafing) and "piecework goldbricking" (that is, quota restriction caused by informal group norms).[41] Like Williams, Roy was always advised to "take it easy."

In addition to these findings, other modern students of labor and management have reached the same conclusions as Whiting Williams, yet apparently without having the benefit of his findings. Based on the contributions of a number of scholars, Sar Levitan concluded that there was "no real blue collar crisis" and that American workers saw themselves as holding middle-class values rather than being of a working class. If there were any "blue collar blues," Levitan continued, they were caused by the rising taxes and inflation that accompanied the welfare state, which the workers resented.[42] Whiting Williams expressed this conclusion just as clearly, and earlier, than Levitan and his experts.

Much more widely recognized among modern students of work is Studs Terkel, who spent three years interviewing numerous workers in a broad spectrum of jobs. His conclusion was that he was "constantly astonished [at how many people] are aware of a sense of personal worth . . . in the work they do."[43] Remarkably, this is the same conclusion that Whiting Williams had reached over fifty years earlier!

John R. Coleman, who worked in blue collar jobs while on a sabbatical from the presidency of Haverford College, recalled that the day he was fired from one of his jobs "hit me hard. I have a secure . . . job to go back to. My family's bills are being paid while I am away. . . .But none of that mattered today. I felt unwanted . . . I wondered why people couldn't see what a valued employee I would be."[44] Williams had stressed how we measured our worth by our job, and Coleman's feelings fit that earlier theme. Or, take the studies of E. E. LeMasters, who became a "regular" in a Milwaukee bar for a period of five years, from 1967 through 1972, to do his research on work and workers. Among his findings was the following statement: "Historically, in Western society the center of a man's life is his job. His self-image, and his status in the community, were reflections of how he earned a living. An unemployed man . . . literally had no position in the society. . . . Even today, when two men meet for the first time, an early question will be: 'What do you do?' "[45] Williams found similar results, although certainly in different surroundings, almost one-half century earlier. LeMasters also criticized modern scholars who view workers as alienated and hating their work (LeMasters focused particularly on Charles A. Reich's *The Greening of America*). LeMasters found such a conclusion to be a myth—just as Whiting Williams had found it so many years before. Even though Williams has not been recognized by the scholars cited above, their modern conclusions are so similar to his that they provide further evidence that Williams was a very perceptive participant-observer.

One student of early behavioral developments, Robert Saltonstall, did give credit to Williams's role in the development of the study of human relations: "Williams succeeded in describing for management, *for the first time*, both the facts of work life and the feelings that lay behind worker attitude and behavior."[46] Otherwise, Williams has received limited recognition for his pioneering studies. Why? One explanation is that his private papers were uncovered only recently at the Western Reserve Historical Society in Cleveland, Ohio. Without primary sources, his background, the factors that influenced his development, and his personal feelings and thoughts could not be examined to provide a perspective on his life and work. A second explanation resides in the fact that he was never connected with an academic institution, except as a visiting lecturer. He had limited academic credentials, wrote for the practitioner, and perhaps lacked the credibility of others who were affiliated academically. Thus, researchers from Harvard University and the Massachusetts Institute of Technology would receive credit for pioneering industrial sociology at the Hawthorne plant of Western Electric even though Williams had preceded them.[47] Academic prestige carries clout and scholars get more credit for citing other scholars than for citing nonacademicians. Finally, perhaps Williams was disregarded because of his lack of research rigor, meaning that he did not use scientifically drawn samples, avoided statistics, and generalized from his experiences and observations. In modern disciplines that aspire to professional standing and robustness, the methods of Williams appear to be irrelevant. Yet the experiences and findings of modern researchers, cited above, bear out Williams's conclusions! Could it be that we choose to ignore findings that run counter to our preconceptions? For example, Levitan and Johnston have challenged the methods and conclusions of modern scholars of work: "Much has been said about the dehumanizing and stultifying impact of work, and there has been no shortage of 'solutions' to the alleged ills. Most of these prescriptions are based, however, on what the reformers know down deep in their hearts. Few have bothered to look at the record."[48] Part of this neglected record is the work of people like Wyckoff, Goehre, Williams, and others who have lived and worked with workers of all types and have recorded their observations.

Even as we examine the record, certain perplexing issues remain: for instance, why do we find Williams's observations of over six decades ago so similar to those findings of recent vintage? Is human nature so unchanging? Perhaps some of the problems change over time, yet there are certain central issues — insecurity, interpersonal relations, human needs for recognition, the desire for pride in work, for example — that do not change in their essence as part of our humanness. The answers to these questions are not apparent, and I am reminded of the phrase *plus ça change, plus c'est la même chose* (the more things change, the more they remain the same.)[49]

Whiting Williams was a pioneer in the study of labor-management relations. His way of obtaining information — as a participant-observer — was unique and effective. He demonstrated that managers really did not know a great deal about their workers, at least from the workers' point of view, nor did the workers know much about management. This mutual ignorance fostered suspicion and mistrust, leading to industrial unrest. The way out was through developing an understanding of the labor-management relationship. Workers should be told of the aims, ideals, and plans of management; they should be recognized and given reasons to have hope and pride; they should be treated in such a manner that they could find self-esteem and the esteem of others in their work. Management needed to use this understanding of workers to develop better human skills and attitudes; to learn to communicate and demonstrate by example the importance of the worker and work in the organization; to give recognition; to build pride; to regularize production to reduce the element of fear; and above all, not to take the worker for granted.

It would have been easy for Whiting Williams to engage in armchair theorizing and philosophizing about what was on the worker's mind. We are indeed fortunate that he did not choose the easy way but instead let the "air blow in this face" as he sought to resolve the causes of industrial unrest. We should study his ideas in order to illuminate our present.

Notes

CHAPTER ONE

1. Abraham J. Baughman, ed., *A Centennial Biographical History of Richland County, Ohio* (Chicago: Lewis Publishing, 1901), pp. 355–56.

2. Autobiographical Notes of Whiting Williams, Williams Papers, Western Reserve Historical Society, Cleveland, Ohio, container 10, folder 5. (Williams's papers occupy 13 containers and have been well organized, preserved, and catalogued by the society's staff.)

3. Williams to Dorothy Hawk, March 25, 1966, Williams Papers, container 3, folder 1. The occasion of this recollection was a return to Shelby to speak to a group of young people in 1966.

4. John Barnard, *From Evangelicalism to Progressivism at Oberlin College, 1866–1917* (Columbus: Ohio State University Press, 1969), pp. 50–51; *see also* Robert S. Fletcher, *A History of Oberlin College* (Oberlin, Ohio: Oberlin College, 1943).

5. Charles Howard Hopkins, *The Rise of The Social Gospel in American Protestantism, 1865–1915* (New Haven: Yale University Press, 1940).

6. Richard D. Knudten, *The Systematic Thought of Washington Gladden* (New York: Humanities Press, 1968); Jacob H. Dorn, *Washington Gladden: Prophet of the Social Gospel* (Columbus: Ohio State University Press, 1966).

7. Barnard, *From Evangelicalism to Progressivism*, p. 62; *see also* John R. Commons, *Social Reform and the Church* (New York: T. Y. Crowell, 1894); John R. Commons, *Myself* (New York: Macmillan, 1934).

8. Autobiographical Notes, container 10, folder 5.

9. "Graham Taylor," *Concise Dictionary of American Biography* (New York: Charles Scribner's Sons, 1980), p. 1024; *see also* John F. McClymer, *War and Welfare: Social Engineering in America: 1890–1925* (Westport, Conn.: Greenwood Press, 1980), pp. 15–20.

10. Barnard, *From Evangelicalism to Progressivism*, pp. 96, 121.

11. Autobiographical Notes, container 10, folder 5.

12. Autobiographical Notes, container 3, folder 1.

13. Autobiographical Notes, container 3, folder 1.

14. Autobiographical Notes, container 10, folder 5.

15. Berlin Diary, Williams Papers, container 5, folder 6.

16. Berlin Diary, container 5, folder 6.

17. Autobiographical Notes, container 10, folder 5.

18. Useful works on Harper and the University of Chicago are Richard J. Storr, *Harper's University: The Beginnings* (Chicago: University of Chi-

cago Press, 1925); Thomas W. Goodspeed *The Story of The University of Chicago, 1890–1925* (Chicago: University of Chicago Press, 1925).

19. Autobiographical Notes, container 10, folder 5.

20. Autobiographical Notes, container 10, folder 5.

21. Autobiographical Notes, container 10, folder 5. In later years, the Reverend Gleason A. Reeder would become president of Baldwin-Wallace College, near Cleveland, Ohio.

22. David N. Keller, *Cooper Industries, 1833–1983* (Athens: Ohio University Press, 1983), p. 27.

23. Autobiographical Notes, container 10, folder 5.

24. Autobiographical Notes, container 10, folder 5.

25. Donald M. Love, *Henry Churchill King of Oberlin* (New Haven: Yale University Press, 1956), p. 230.

26. Henry C. King to Williams, November 17, 1904, container 1, folder 1.

27. James H. Fairchild, *Oberlin: The Colony and the College* (Oberlin, Ohio: E. J. Goodrich, 1883), p. 267.

28. Harter Whiting Williams to author, February 28, 1984. Harter Williams explained the "Uneeda cookie box glass door" as a "contraption which could be moved from one cookie box to the next as the cookies were sold." What Whiting Williams observed the Wright brothers doing with their study of tobacco smoke curling over and under the plane wing is an early concept of a wind tunnel.

29. Charles Whiting Williams, "The Scientific Study of the College Student," *Science* 38 (1913): 114–20; Charles Whiting Williams, "How May the Problems of University and College Best Be Studied?" *Religious Education* 7 (1912): 386–90; Charles Whiting Williams, "Commerce and the Campus," *Saturday Evening Post*, February 25, 1911, pp. 12–13, 42; Charles Whiting Williams, "His All-Round Excellency: The College President," *The Independent* 74 (1913): 499–503.

30. Morrell Heald, *The Social Responsibilities of Business: Company and Community, 1900–1960* (Cleveland: Case Western Reserve University Press, 1970), p. 25.

31. C[harles] W[hiting] Williams, "Cleveland's Group Plan," *Survey* 29 (1913): 603–06; Charles Whiting Williams, "Cleveland's Federated Givers," *The American Review of Reviews* 48 (1913): 472–75; Charles Whiting Williams, "The Forlorn Philanthropist: Is It More Blessed to Give Than to Receive?" *Saturday Evening Post*, December 20, 1913, pp. 31–34; Charles Whiting Williams, "City Planning in Flesh and Blood," *National Municipal Review* 8 (1919): 466–71. Material on the Cleveland Welfare Federation, successor to the Cleveland Federation for Charity and Philanthropy, may be found in the Williams Papers, container 11, folder 3.

32. Heald, *The Social Responsibilities of Business,* p. 25; *see also* pp. 117–22, 155–58 for information on the emergence and growth of community chest associations.

33. John E. Barber to Williams, May 15, 1956, container 3, folder 1.

34. Autobiographical Notes, container 5, folder 2; Dorothy Rogers Williams, personal conversation, August 19, 1982.

35. Charles W. Williams to Probate Court of Cuyahoga County, Cleve-

land, Ohio, June 19, 1917. For "simplicity and avoidance of confusion," the petition to change his name was granted. Williams Papers, container 1, folder 1.

36. The Hydraulic Pressed Steel Company merged with Truscon Steel of Youngstown, Ohio, in 1931; Truscon merged with the Republic Steel Corporation in 1935. The remains of the Hydraulic Pressed Steel Company exist as the division of the Republic Steel Corporation that serves the automotive trades in the Cleveland area. William G. Rose, *Cleveland: The Making of a City* (New York: World Publishing Company, 1950), p. 882.

37. Alfred D. Chandler, Jr., *The Visible Hand* (Cambridge: Harvard University Press, 1977), p. 9.

38. For further information on the position of "social secretary," *see* William H. Tolman, *Social Engineering* (New York: McGraw, 1909), pp. 48–59; *see also* Stuart D. Brandes, *American Welfare Capitalism: 1890–1940* (Chicago: University of Chicago Press, 1976); Daniel Nelson, *Managers and Workers: Origins of the New Factory System in the United States: 1880–1920* (Madison: University of Wisconsin Press, 1975), chap. 6.

39. Frederick W. Taylor, *Shop Management* (New York: Harper and Row, 1903); Frederick W. Taylor, *The Principles of Scientific Management* (New York: Harper and Row, 1911); both reissued as part of Frederick W. Taylor, *Scientific Management* (New York: Harper and Row, 1947).

40. Robert F. Lovett, "Present Tendencies in Personnel Practice," *Industrial Management* 65 (1923): 327–33.

41. Whiting Williams, *Human Relations in Industry* (Washington, D.C.: U.S. Department of Labor, 1918), pp. 9–10. Williams was among the first, and perhaps the very first, to cast this focus on employee-employer relations into the idea of "human relations" in industry. Another early expression of these ideas can be found in Robert B. Wolf, "The Human Relations in Industry" (address delivered to the Associated Industries of Massachusetts, Boston, Mass., October 23, 1919).

42. Whiting Williams, "What Every Worker Wants" (pamphlet), p. 1. I am indebted to Fred Kersting of Dallas, Texas, for this material.

43. Allan H. Mogensen recorded a series of Williams's lectures at the Work Simplification Conferences, Lake Placid, N.Y., in 1960, 1961, and 1962. Mr. Mogensen has the original tapes, but he kindly permitted me to make copies, which are in the Harry W. Bass Business History Collection at the University of Oklahoma. There are eight cassettes and this quote is from cassette number 3, recorded July 24, 1961, Lake Placid, N.Y.

44. Walter A. Wyckoff, *The Workers: The East* (New York: Charles Scribner's Sons, 1897); Walter A. Wyckoff, *The Workers: The West* (New York: Charles Scribner's Sons, 1898). Walter A. Wyckoff (1865–1908) was the son of a minister of the Social Gospel persuasion; *see Who Was Who in America* (Chicago: Marquis, 1942), vol. 1, p. 1387.

45. His findings were published first in German, as Paul Goehre, *Drei Monate Fabrikarbeiter und Handwerkburche* (Leipzig: F. W. Grunow, 1891); and in English as *Three Months in a Workshop* (London: Swan Sonnenschein, 1895). An excellent summary of Goehre's ideas may be found in Richard J. Whiting, "Historical Search in Human Relations," *Academy of Management Journal* 7 (1964): 45–53.

46. Henry A. Roemer to Williams, December 3, 1963, container 3, folder 1. At the time, Roemer was general manager of the Canton Sheet Steel Division of the Hydraulic Pressed Steel Company; later, Roemer started his own company, Sharon Steel, of Sharon, Pa.

CHAPTER TWO

1. Williams Tapes, Harry W. Bass Business History Collection, University of Oklahoma, Norman, cassette number 2, July 24, 1961.

2. Williams Tapes, cassette number 2, July 24, 1961.

3. Whiting Williams, *What's on the Worker's Mind: By One Who Put on Overalls to Find Out* (New York: Charles Scribner's Sons, 1920), p. v. Parts of this book were published earlier in a *Collier's* series entitled "What the Worker Thinks," 65 (1920): 9–10, 25; 65 (1920): 10–11, 47–49; 65 (1920): 10–11, 60, 62; 66 (1920): 7, 36–40.

4. Robert K. Murray, *Red Scare: A Study in National Hysteria, 1919–1920* (Minneapolis: University of Minnesota Press, 1955), chap. 7; also helpful is William E. Leuchtenburg, *The Perils of Prosperity, 1914–32* (Chicago: University of Chicago Press, 1958), chap. 4.

5. *U.S. Commission on Industrial Relations: Final Report* (Washington, D.C.: U.S. Government Printing Office, 1915), especially pp. 23–91. *See also* Mark Perlman, *Labor Union Theories in America* (Evanston, Illinois: Row, Peterson, and Company), pp. 279–304.

6. Quoted in Ray Stannard Baker, *The New Industrial Unrest: Reasons and Remedies* (Garden City, N.Y.: Doubleday, 1920), p. 52. Baker, a "muckraker," was a close friend and a biographer of President Wilson.

7. Valerie Jean Conner, *The National War Labor Board* (Chapel Hill: University of North Carolina Press, 1983). The seeds planted by the NWLB would bear fruit for more than half a century through legislation such as the National Labor Relations Act (NLRA), the Fair Labor Standards Act (FLSA), and the Equal Pay Amendment to the FLSA.

8. Murray, *Red Scare*, pp. 7–9; David Brody, *Labor in Crisis: The Steel Strike of 1919* (New York: J. B. Lippincott, 1965); Robert H. Zieger, *Republicans and Labor: 1919-1929* (Lexington: University of Kentucky Press, 1969), pp. 8–22.

9. Williams, *What's on the Worker's Mind*, p. v.

10. *ARMCO, The First Twenty Years* (Middletown, Ohio: ARMCO, 1922), cited in Daniel Nelson, *Managers and Workers: Origins of the New Factory System in the U.S.* (Madison: University of Wisconsin Press, 1975), p. 79.

11. Williams, *What's on the Worker's Mind?* p. 14.

12. Williams, *What's on the Worker's Mind?* pp. 16–17.

13. Williams, *What's on the Worker's Mind?* p. 282.

14. Williams, *What's on the Worker's Mind?* p. 33.

15. Williams, *What's on the Worker's Mind?* p. 299.

16. Williams, *What's on the Worker's Mind?* p. 299.

17. Williams, *What's on the Worker's Mind?* p. 225. In some versions of

the story, Williams added the sentence: "A bum neither rides nor walks nor works."

18. Williams Tapes, cassette number 2, July 24, 1961.

19. Williams, *What's on the Worker's Mind?* p. 289.

20. Whiting Williams, "The Job and Utopia," *American Labor Legislation Review* 11 (1921): 19.

21. Williams, *What's on the Worker's Mind?* p. 284.

22. Selig Perlman, *A Theory of the Labor Movement* (New York: Macmillan, 1928).

23. Williams, "The Job and Utopia," p. 16.

24. Williams, *What's on the Worker's Mind?* p. 15.

25. Williams, *What's on the Worker's Mind?* p. 283.

26. Williams, *What's on the Worker's Mind?* p. 284.

27. Whiting Williams, "'More Production?'—Say, Where D'Ya Get That Stuff?" *Annals of the American Academy of Political and Social Science* 89 (1920): 180.

28. Josephine Goldmark, *Fatigue and Efficiency* (New York: Russell Sage Foundation, 1912), p. 174.

29. Douglas McGregor, *The Human Side of Enterprise* (New York: McGraw-Hill, 1960), pp. 16–18.

30. Williams, "The Job and Utopia," p. 22.

31. Williams, *What's on the Worker's Mind?* p. 323.

32. *See* Ordway Tead, *Instincts in Industry: A Study of Working Class Psychology* (Boston: Houghton-Mifflin, 1918); a summary of the notion of instincts as forces animating human behavior may be found in Daniel A. Wren, *The Evolution of Management Thought* (New York: John Wiley and Sons, 1979), pp. 210–11.

33. Whiting Williams, "What Makes the Human Wheels Go Round," *100%*, February 1920, pp. 59–60, 63–64; Whiting Williams, "Human Nature Abhors the Cipher," *100%*, March 1920, pp. 72, 74, 118.

34. *See* Paul H. Douglas, *The Theory of Wages* (New York: Macmillan, 1934), pp. 270–72; Richard A. Lester, *The Economics of Labor* (New York: Macmillan, 1941), p. 104.

35. Williams, *What's on the Worker's Mind?* p. 39. (Emphasis added by Williams.)

36. Williams, *What's on the Worker's Mind?* p. 179.

37. Williams, "What the Worker Thinks," p. 10.

38. Williams, "What the Worker Thinks," p. 49.

39. Williams, "What the Worker Thinks," p. 50.

40. Williams, *What's on the Worker's Mind?* p. 148.

41. Williams, *What's on the Worker's Mind?* p. 281.

42. Williams, *What's on the Worker's Mind?* p. 81.

CHAPTER THREE

1. Autobiographical Notes of Whiting Williams, Williams Papers, Western Reserve Historical Society, Cleveland, Ohio, container 1, folder 1.

2. John R. Commons et al., *History of Labour in the United States*, 4 vols. (New York: Macmillan, 1918), 2: 179, 495–97.

3. Whiting Williams, *What's on the Worker's Mind: By One Who Put On Overalls to Find Out* (New York: Charles Scribner's Sons, 1920), p. 155.

4. Williams, *What's on the Worker's Mind?* p. 155.

5. Williams to J. H. Foster (president of the Hydraulic Pressed Steel Company), April 1, 1919, Williams Papers, container 1, folder 1. Williams's italics. The reference to "Carnegie Steel" was incorrect—Andrew Carnegie had sold out to J. P. Morgan and his colleagues in 1900. After that, the proper name of the company was the U.S. Steel Corporation, not Carnegie Steel, although some people still connected Carnegie with the new company.

6. Whiting Williams to Ernest E. Bell (vice-president of the Hydraulic Pressed Steel Company), July 8, 1919, container 3, folder 4.

7. David Brody, *Labor in Crisis: The Steel Strike of 1919* (New York: J. B. Lippincott, 1965), pp. 78–79.

8. Whiting Williams, "'Labor Unrest' as Seen by a Steel Official Who Shoveled Soot," *Literary Digest* 65 (1920): 78–84.

9. Williams to Elbert H. Gary, August 19, 1919, container 1, folder 1.

10. Ida Tarbell, *The Life of Elbert H. Gary* (New York: Appleton, 1925), pp. 282–83.

11. Brody, *Labor in Crisis*, pp. 136–43. An investigation of Foster did disclose his agitation to overthrow the capitalistic system by "boring from within" through the legitimate labor union movement. Perlman and Taft, however, maintain that Foster had a radical "past" but had helped sell Liberty Bonds during the war as a patriot. *See* Selig Perlman and Phillip Taft, *History of Labor in the United States, 1896-1932* (New York: Macmillan, 1935), p. 466. Foster resigned, but too late to help the striking forces. Foster, in retrospect, laid the blame for the strike's failure on organized labor itself. The strike committee quarreled internally over which craft union would represent which workers, and the main body of organized labor failed to back the committee. *See* William Z. Foster, *The Great Steel Strike and Its Lessons* (New York: B. W. Huebsch, 1920), pp. 234–54. In 1932, this "patriot" who had sold Liberty Bonds ran for president of the United States as the candidate of the Communist party.

12. John P. Frey to Alfred Todd, Iron Founder's Society, Manchester, England, May 13, 1920, container 1, folder 1; Harlow S. Person to Margaret G. Bonfield, secretary of the National Federation of Women Workers, Trade Union Congress, London, England, June 14, 1920, container 1, folder 1.

13. Whiting Williams, *Full Up and Fed Up: The Worker's Mind in Crowded Britain* (New York: Charles Scribner's Sons, 1921), p. 90.

14. Whiting Williams, "The Job and Utopia," *American Labor Legislation Review* 2 (1921): 20.

15. Whiting Williams, "Ingots, Pigs, and Men," *Survey* 45 (1921): 799–807. *See also* Whiting Williams, "I'll Work Here!" *Collier's* 66 (1920): 7, 23–26.

16. Williams, *Full Up and Fed Up*, p. 119.

17. Williams, *Full Up and Fed Up*, p. 207.

18. Williams, "Ingots, Pigs, and Men," pp. 799–807. *See also* Williams, "I'll Work Here!"

19. Williams, *Full Up and Fed Up*, p. 166.

20. Williams, *Full Up and Fed Up*, p. 159.
21. Whiting Williams, "Full Up," *Scribner's* 69 (1921): 410. Perhaps it was Williams's foresight, or perhaps my hindsight, but his observation about "initiative and progress" and its role in economic development antedates the research of David McClelland, John Atkinson, and others on the "need for achievement" in society. McClelland found that the British, who in the past were high in the need for achievement, had lost that drive in the twentieth century and that this contributed to their economic stagnation. *See* David C. McClelland, "Business Drive and National Achievement," *Harvard Business Review* 40 (1962): 108; *see also* David C. McClelland, *The Achieving Society* (New York: John Wiley and Sons, 1961), especially pp. 132–49.
22. Horace King Hathaway to Henri le Chatelier (a leading French advocate of scientific management); Samuel Gompers to Leon Jouhaux of the *Confédération Générale du Travail;* Herbert Hoover to John R. Clynes, House of Commons; and Governor Davis "to whom it may concern," container 1, folders 1 and 2.
23. Whiting Williams, *Horny Hands and Hampered Elbows: The Worker's Mind in Western Europe* (New York: Charles Scribner's Sons, 1922); a prepublication summary appeared as Whiting Williams, "Europe at Work," *Scribner's* 71 (1922): 131–44; 71 (1922): 320–33; 71 (1922): 451–64.
24. Williams, *Horny Hands and Hampered Elbows*, p. 266.
25. Williams, "Europe at Work," pp. 131–44, 320–33.
26. Williams, "Europe at Work," p. 460.

CHAPTER FOUR

1. Whiting Williams, "When a Man's Laid Off," *Collier's* 67 (1921): 7–8, 21. Williams, by today's standards, was chauvinistic about women at work. He felt that work was a "means" to a woman rather than an "end"; that is, a woman did not measure her self-worth by her job. He did, however, note that times were changing with more educational chances for females to make their work more challenging and more important. *See* Whiting Williams, "What's on the Working Woman's Mind," *Scribner's* 85 (1929): 460–66; Whiting Williams, "The Ex-Cradle Rocker and Her Club," *Scribner's* 80 (1926): 539–44.
2. Whiting Williams, "The Worker and The Church: Getting Apart and Getting Together," *in Business and the Church*, ed. Jerome Davis (New York: The Century Company, 1926), pp. 79–89; Whiting Williams, "The Spiritual Side of the Labor Problem," *Literary Digest* 98 (1928): 29–30.
3. Whiting Williams, "The Job and Utopia," *American Labor Legislation Review* 11 (1921): 22. *See also* Whiting Williams, "Say It with Jobs," *Collier's* 68 (1921): 4–7, 22–23; Whiting Williams, "A Job for Every Man Every Day," *Collier's* 69 (1922): 9–10, 21.
4. Phillip Taft, *The AF of L in the Time of Gompers* (New York: Harper and Row, 1957), p. 366. For the opposition to Gompers, *see* James O. Morris, *Conflict within the AFL* (Ithaca: Cornell University Press, 1958), pp. 44, 105. Another useful work is Daniel Nelson, *Unemployment Insurance: The American Experience, 1915–1935* (Madison: University of Wisconsin Press, 1969).
5. Williams, "When a Man's Laid Off." *See also* H[erman] Feldman,

The Regularization of Employment (New York: Harper and Row, 1925).

6. Robert K. Murray, "Herbert Hoover and the Harding Cabinet," *in Herbert Hoover as Secretary of Commerce,* ed. Ellis W. Hawley (Iowa City: University of Iowa Press, 1981), pp. 24–25, 57–59; Robert H. Zieger, *Republicans and Labor* (Lexington: University of Kentucky Press, 1969), pp. 91–96.

7. *See* Edward Berman, *Labor Disputes and the President of the United States* (New York: Columbia University Press, 1924), pp. 155–57.

8. At this time there were sixteen recognized railway labor organizations: the five "operating" unions were the "brotherhoods," whose members ran the trains (firemen, engineers, brakemen, etc.); the eleven "nonoperating" unions serviced and maintained the engines, cars, tracks, and stations. The brotherhoods were established earlier and were stronger, while the nonoperating groups were affiliated with the AFL's Railway Employees Department (representing craftsmen such as blacksmiths, boilermakers, and machinists), and were of more recent origin.

9. Selig Perlman and Robert Taft, *History of Labor in the United States, 1896–1932* (New York: Macmillan, 1935), pp. 513–20; Taft, *AF of L,* pp. 404–6, 472–474; Richard A. Lester, *Labor Economics* (New York: Macmillan, 1941), pp. 771–74.

10. Edward Hungerford, *Daniel Willard Rides the Line* (New York: G. P. Putnam's Sons, 1938).

11. Whiting Williams, "Why My Buddies Will Strike Again," *Collier's* 70 (1922): 12.

12. Williams, "Why My Buddies," p. 13.

13. Williams, "Why My Buddies," p. 15.

14. Williams, "Why My Buddies," p. 13.

15. Williams to Daniel Willard, president of the B&O Railroad, August 7, 1922, Williams Papers, Western Reserve Historical Society, Cleveland, Ohio, container 3, folder 4. Williams referred to Willard as an example of what a leader should be. In one instance, he quoted Willard that "all men get paid about the same on the different railroads, but some [companies] make money, and some don't—the difference is in the leadership—getting people to work with you." Williams Tapes, Harry W. Bass Business History Collection, University of Oklahoma, Norman, cassette number 2, July 24, 1961.

16. Williams to Daniel Willard, September 26, 1922, container 3, folder 4.

17. Harter Whiting Williams to author, February 1, 1982. The actual letter that Williams carried was not found among his papers. Its existence is verified, however, in a letter of July 14, 1923, from Samuel Gompers to Williams, container 1, folder 2.

18. Whiting Williams, "In the Strike Breaker's Camp," *Collier's* 70 (1922): 9–10.

19. Williams, "In the Strike Breaker's Camp," p. 10.

20. Williams, "In the Strike Breaker's Camp," p. 9.

21. Williams, "In the Strike Breaker's Camp," p. 10.

22. Whiting Williams, "What I Know Now about Railroader's," *Collier's* 70 (1922): 29.

23. Williams, "What I Know Now," p. 29.

24. Williams, "What I Know Now," p. 13.

25. Williams, "What I Know Now," p. 13.

26. *See* Berman, *Labor Disputes,* pp. 239–40; Louis A. Wood, *Union-Management Cooperation on the Railroads* (New Haven: Yale University Press, 1931), pp. 76–78.

27. Marguerite Green, *The National Civic Federation and the American Labor Movement, 1900–1925* (Washington, D.C.: Catholic University Press, 1956).

28. Milton J. Nadworny, *Scientific Management and the Unions, 1900–1932* (Cambridge: Harvard University Press, 1955), pp. 122–41; Morris, *Conflict within the AFL,* pp. 55–56; Daniel A. Wren, *The Evolution of Management Thought* (New York: John Wiley and Sons, 1979), pp. 169–71.

29. For the "Rochester Plan" in the clothing industry, *see* Meyer Jacobstein, "Can Industrial Democracy Be Efficient? The Rochester Plan," *in Scientific Management Since Taylor,* ed. E. E. Hunt (New York: McGraw-Hill, 1924), pp. 212–21; Daniel Willard, "The New Executive Viewpoint on Labor Relations," *Industrial Management* 73 (1927): 260–63; Otto S. Beyer, Jr., "Experiences with Cooperation between Labor and Management in the Railway Industry," *in Wertheim Lectures on Industrial Relations,* (Cambridge: Harvard University Press, 1929).

30. *See* "Results of Cooperation of Workers and Management on the Railroads," *Monthly Labor Review* 25 (1927): 30–33.

31. Whiting Williams, "How'd You Like to be a Labor Leader?" *Collier's* 71 (1923): 5–6.

32. Williams to Daniel Willard, September 26, 1922, container 3, folder 4. A company magazine was established, but the idea of the company song was not implemented.

33. Whiting Williams, "Let's Try to Get Along With Them," *Collier's* 75 (1924): 11–12.

34. U.S. Department of Labor, *Proceedings of the First Industrial Conference, October 6–23, 1919, and Report of the [Second] Industrial Conference, December 1, 1919–March 6, 1920* (Washington, D.C.: U.S. Government Printing Office, 1920). *See also* Haggai Hurvitz, "Ideology and Industrial Conflict: President Wilson's First Industrial Conference of October, 1919," *Labor History* 18 (1977): 509–24; Gary Dean Best, "President Wilson's Second Industrial Conference, 1919–1920," *Labor History* 16 (1975): 505–20.

35. Robert H. Zieger, "Herbert Hoover, the Wage Earner and the 'New Economic System,' 1919–1929," *in Herbert Hoover as Secretary of Commerce,* ed. Ellis W. Hawley (Iowa City: University of Iowa Press, 1981), pp. 84–85, 96–98.

36. Herbert Hoover to Williams, February 17, 1921, container 1, folder 1. Other prominent supporters of the shop councils were Cyrus S. Ching and Mary Parker Follett. Ching, director of industrial relations for U.S. Rubber and later director of the Federal Mediation and Conciliation Service, gave his views in *Review and Reflection* (New York: B. C. Forbes, 1953), pp. 25–34. The views of Follett, a pioneer in seeking how to resolve conflict, can be

found in H. C. Metcalf and L. Urwick, eds., *Dynamic Administration: The Collected Papers of Mary Parker Follett* (New York: Harper and Row, 1940), pp. 177–79.

37. Mary Follett, a contemporary of Williams, was a supporter of the B&O plan and the shop councils. On the matter of authority, she noted that the "aim of employee representation . . . should be not to share power, but to increase power"; that is, worker participation did not split or lessen management's authority, but increased the authority of the whole organization. *See* Metcalf and Urwick, *Dynamic Administration*, p. 182.

38. Williams Tapes, cassette number 4, July 24, 1961.

39. For an example, see the study of the Dutchess Bleachery, Wappingers Fall, New York, *in* Ben M. Selekman, *Sharing Management with the Worker* (New York: Russell Sage Foundation, 1924). The foreword outlines the projects under study. Another example, a longitudinal case study, is Robert Ozanne, *A Century of Labor-Management Relations at McCormick and International Harvester* (Madison: University of Wisconsin Press, 1967).

40. H. B. Butler, *Industrial Relations in the U.S.* (Geneva: International Labor Office, 1927), pp. 84–105; *see also* Norman J. Wood, "Industrial Relations Policies of American Management, 1900–1933," *Business History Review* 34 (1960): 403–20.

41. For this and other evaluations of the shop council movement see Milton Derber, *The American Idea of Industrial Democracy, 1865–1965* (Urbana: University of Illinois Press, 1970), pp. 219–29. A more positive evaluation may be found in Daniel Nelson, "The Company Union Movement, 1900–1937: A Reexamination," *Business History Review* 56 (1982): 335–57.

42. Whiting Williams, *Full Up and Fed Up: The Worker's Mind in Crowded Britain* (New York: Charles Scribner's Sons, 1921), pp. 117–18.

43. Richard T. Ely, *The Labor Movement in America* (New York: T. Y. Crowell and Company, 1886), p. ix.

44. James H. Timberlake, *Prohibition and the Progressive Movement, 1900–1920* (Cambridge: Harvard University Press, 1963); Jacob Henry Dorn, *Washington Gladden: Prophet of the Social Gospel* (Columbus: Ohio State University Press, 1966); Herbert Asbury, *The Great Illusion: An Informal History of Prohibition* (Garden City, N.Y.: Doubleday, 1950).

45. Dorothy Rogers Williams, personal conversation, August 1982, Cleveland, Ohio. (Even then, Williams restricted his alcoholic intake to a "light sherry after dinner.")

46. Whiting Williams, "John Barleycorn and the Worker," *Collier's* 68 (1921): 5. *See also* Williams, "What Is on the Worker's Mind?" *Proceedings of the National Conference of Social Work* (Chicago: University of Chicago Press, 1921), p. 33.

47. Williams, "John Barleycorn and the Worker," p. 6.

48. Williams, "John Barleycorn and the Worker," p. 26.

49. Whiting Williams, "Sober and Glad of It," *Collier's* 70 (1922): 29. Williams also felt that Prohibition would reduce collisions between railroad locomotives and automobiles since there were too many drinking drivers among the two and one-half million cars then on the American roads. *See* Whiting Williams, "How'd You Like to be the Engineer?" *Collier's* 75 (1925): 18, 41.

50. William Green to Williams, April 27, 1922, container 1, folder 1; M. F. Tighe to Williams, April 24, 1922, container 1, folder 1.

51. Taft, *AF of L,* p. 465.

52. Timberlake, *Prohibition and the Progressive Movement,* pp. 70–80.

53. The board of directors held some prominent names, for example: Frank Gannett, New York publisher; F. J. Harwood, a Wisconsin manufacturer whose factory became a testing ground for human relations ideas; James C. Penney, merchant; and Amos Alonzo Stagg, director of athletics at the University of Chicago. Extensive correspondence between this group and Williams may be found in container 1, folder 3.

54. Whiting Williams, "Workers' Speakeasy," *Survey* 65 (1931): 493–95, 528; Whiting Williams, "Yes, My Workers Are Drier, But – ," *Survey* 68 (1932): 213–16, 242–44.

CHAPTER FIVE

1. Williams to Daniel Willard, July 25, 1924, Williams Papers, Western Reserve Historical Society, Cleveland, Ohio, container 3, folder 4.

2. *See* [Whiting Williams], "The 'Whys' Man of the B&O," *Business Week,* March 1, 1930, p. 39; Williams to Willard, June 14, 1941, container 4, folder 3.

3. Williams to D. C. Harper, vice-president of Standard Oil of New York, June 20, 1939, container 4, folder 2.

4. Williams to H. Wilkinson, vice-presidentof Shell Oil Corporation, June 20, 1939; container 4, folder 2. For more information on Shell and its personnel practices, *see* Kendall Beaton, *Enterprise in Oil: A History of Shell in the United States* (New York: Appleton-Century-Crofts, 1957), especially pp. 101–2, 487–92.

5. Theodore V. Purcell, *The Worker Speaks His Mind on Company and Union* (Cambridge: Harvard University Press, 1953), pp. 47–51.

6. Williams to W. B. Traynor, October 21, 1925, container 3, folder 4.

7. Williams to T. H. Dillon, April 16, 1927; September 20, 1927; and June 15, 1928; all in container 3, folder 4. *See also* Stacy May and Galo Plaza, *The United Fruit Company in Latin America* (Washington, D.C.: National Planning Association, 1958), pp. 188–200.

8. *Western Electric News* 10 (1921): 22; *Western Electric News* 11 (1922): 14.

9. *Western Electric News* 9 (1920): 7; *Western Electric News* 9 (1921): 12–14.

10. Whiting Williams to H. A. Halligan, December 15, 1922, container 3, folder 4.

11. Williams to H. A. Halligan, January 5, 1923, container 3, folder 4. On this trip to New York, Williams was paid $1,500 for three weeks of work, plus travel and living expenses. In this report, Williams named the individuals with whom he spoke while in New York: "Messrs. DuBois, Houston, Carty, Hill, Pingree, Gilman, and Bergquist." I am indebted to Mary Jo Jones, Western Electric Company Librarian, for identifying Charles Gilbert DuBois as Western Electric president from 1919 through 1926; John Joseph Carty as

a vice-president of American Telephone & Telegraph; George E. Pingree as vice-president of Western Electric International; and Carl W. Bergquist as chairman of the Personnel Committee from 1922 through 1928 and later as head of public relations at the Hawthorne plants. The others could not be identified from company archives. (Mary Jo Jones to author, October 7, 1982.)

12. Ronald G. Greenwood, Alfred A. Bolton, and Regina A. Greenwood, "Hawthorne a Half Century Later: Relay Assembly Participants Remember," *Journal of Management* 9 (1983): 222.

13. Greenwood, Bolton, and Greenwood, "Hawthorne a Half Century Later," p. 222.

14. Professor Ronald G. Greenwood, personal conversation, March 8, 1984.

15. Williams to the chairman of the Personnel Committee, Western Electric Company, August 25, 1923, container 3, folder 4.

16. *Western Electric News* 12 (1923): 22.

17. Williams to the Personnel Committee, Western Electric Company, November 21, 1923, container 3, folder 4. For this assignment, Williams received $1,000 plus $100 for expenses.

18. Albert James Beatty, *Corporation Schools* (Bloomington, Ill.: Public School Publishing, 1918), p. 79, 119–20; John V. L. Morris, *Employee Training: A Study of Education and Training Departments in Various Corporations* (New York: McGraw-Hill, 1921), pp. 37–52.

19. *Western Electric News* 13 (1924): 21.

20. Williams to H. A. Halligan, vice-president, Western Electric Company, July 10, 1924, container 3, folder 4.

21. J. W. Dietz, "Some Aspects of Personnel Research in a Manufacturing Organization," *The Annals of the American Academy* 119 (1925): 103–7. At that time (1925) Dietz was secretary of the Personnel Committee.

22. Laurence Whyte, "50th Anniversary—Hawthorne Studies," undated document provided by Robert Sloan of Western Electric, pp. 36–37.

23. Burleigh B. Gardner to author, February 13, 1984. Dr. Gardner is currently chairman of the board of Social Research, Inc., Chicago, Illinois.

24. Stanley S. Holmes, "Extra Incentive Wage Plans Used by the Hawthorne Works of the Western Electric Company" (address delivered before the American Management Association, May 21, 1925); cited in Ordway Tead and Henry C. Metcalf, *Personnel Administration* (New York: McGraw-Hill, 1926), p. 326.

25. An excellent reference on these studies is Charles D. Wrege, "Facts and Fallacies of Hawthorne: A Historical Study of the Origins, Procedures and Results of the Hawthorne Illumination Tests and Their Influence on the Hawthorne Studies" (Ph.D. diss., New York University, 1961).

26. George A. Pennock, "Test Studies in Industrial Research at Hawthorne," *in* Western Electric Co., *Research Studies in Employee Effectiveness and Industrial Relations* (papers presented for the Conference of the Personnel Research Federation, November 15, 1929). Literature on the Hawthorne experiments has become vast. For more information, *see* Elton Mayo, *The Human Problems of an Industrial Civilization* (New York: Macmillan, 1933), pp. 55–69; Fritz J. Roethlisberger and William J. Dickson,

Management and the Worker (Cambridge: Harvard University Press, 1939), pp. 15–86.

27. Cited by C. D. Wrege, "Facts and Fallacies of Hawthorne," p. 2.

CHAPTER SIX

1. Thomas L. Wheelen and J. David Hunger, "Graduate Business Education—75th Anniversary, 1900–1975," *Journal of Management* 1 (1975), 51–53.

2. F. Humervell, secretary of the President and Fellows of Harvard College, to Williams, June 3, 1920, Williams Papers, Western Reserve Historical Society, Cleveland, Ohio, container 1, folder 1.

3. Melvin T. Copeland, *And Mark an Era* (Boston: Little, Brown and Company, 1958), pp. 179–83. *See also* Herbert Heaton, *A Scholar in Action: Edwin F. Gay* (New York: Greenwood Press, 1968), especially pp. 67–81.

4. Howard Elliott to W. B. Donham, June 16, 1922, and November 3, 1923. I am indebted to Professor Emil Walter-Busch, University of St. Gallen, Switzerland, for providing these references from the Harvard University Archives, September 21, 1983.

5. W. B. Donham to Howard Elliott, April 26, 1922. Letter provided to author by Professor Emil Walter-Busch.

6. Washburn to W. B. Donham, January 11, 1922. Letter provided to author by Professor Emil Walter-Busch.

7. W. B. Donham to Hughes, December 12, 1922. Again, I am indebted to Professor Walter-Busch whose research on Donham led to these additional insights into Whiting Williams.

8. Correspondence relating to these lectures is in container 3, folder 2.

9. Lecture notes for November 12, 1925, Harvard class, Williams Papers, container 10, folder 1.

10. Charles W. Eliot to Williams, February 3, 1922, container 1, folder 1.

11. The file of lectures for Dartmouth and Harvard shows that Williams spoke from a topical outine, filling in as he proceeded, *see* container 10, folder 1. *See also* Whiting Williams, "Management and Human Relations," *The Amos Tuck School Clearing House Review* 2 (1923): 7–10.

12. Eugene Gay-Tifft, "Head and Shoulders: The Careers of Whiting Williams" (undated manuscript), Williams Papers, container 2, folder 1.

13. Ernest M. Hopkins to Williams, June 29, 1921, container 1, folder 1.

14. James C. Worthy to author, September 10, 1983. Dr. Worthy's career has included positions as a partner of Cresap, McCormick and Paget, management consultants; vice-president of Sears, Roebuck and Company; and assistant secretary of commerce of the United States of America. He is currently a professor at the Kellogg Graduate School of Management, Northwestern University, Evanston, Illinois.

15. Williams Papers, container 9, folders 1–4 and container 10, folders 1, 6, and 7. (These folders contain copies of these talks and provide an idea of the topics and the groups to whom they were given.)

16. Whiting Williams, *Mainsprings of Men* (New York: Charles Scribner's Sons, 1925), p. v. Before this book was published, portions were serialized in Whiting Williams, "Mainsprings of Men," *Scribner's* 73 (1923): 90–96, 233–40, 346–47, 489–96. Similar conclusions may also be found in Whiting Williams, "What the Worker Wants in His Work," *The Foremen's Magazine* 2 (1926): 6–7.

17. Williams, *Mainsprings of Men*, p. vi.

18. Whiting Williams, "What's Machinery Doing to Us?" *in Problems of Civilization*, ed. Ellsworth Huntington (New York: D. Van Nostrand, 1929), p. 58.

19. *See* Daniel A. Wren, *The Evolution of Management Thought* (New York: John Wiley and Sons, 1979), pp. 210–11, for a summary of this notion of human motivation. These instinct theorists were not too far removed from the phrenologists, graphologists, and other pseudopsychologists of the early twentieth century.

20. Williams, *Mainsprings of Men*, p. 144.

21. Williams, *Mainsprings of Men*, p. 146.

22. Williams, *Mainsprings of Men*, p. 147.

23. Williams, *What's on the Worker's Mind: By One Who Put on Overalls to Find Out* (New York: Charles Scribner's Sons, 1920), pp. 72–73.

24. Williams, *Mainsprings of Men*, p. 27. The idea that humans are motivated to satisfy certain needs (rather than being driven by instincts) appeared in 1938; *see* Henry H. Murray, *Explorations in Personality* (New York: Oxford University Press, 1938). In 1943, Abraham H. Maslow proposed a theoretical hierarchy of needs from the most basic, "physiological," upward through safety, love, esteem and self-actualization." *See* Abraham H. Maslow, "A Theory of Human Motivation," *Psychological Review* 50 (1943): 370–96.

25. Williams, *Mainsprings of Men*, p. 42.

26. Williams, *Mainsprings of Men*, pp. 27–28.

27. Williams, *Mainsprings of Men*, p. 201.

28. Williams, *Mainsprings of Men*, p. 58. Williams's capital letters.

29. Whiting Williams, "Who's Got Momma's Ear?" *Nations Business* 38 (1946): 41.

30. Whiting Williams, "What's on the Working Woman's Mind?" *Scribner's* 85 (1929): 460.

31. Williams, "What's on the Working Woman's Mind?" pp. 463–66.

32. Williams, *Mainsprings of Men*, p. 180.

33. Williams, *Mainsprings of Men*, p. 62.

34. Whiting Williams, "Theory of Industrial Conduct and Leadership," *Harvard Business Review* 1 (1923): 326.

35. Williams, *Mainsprings of Men*, p. 60.

36. This version of an oft-told tale is from Whiting Williams, "The World's Got to Have Me!" *The North American Review* 228 (1929): 449.

37. Whiting Williams, "What's Big Business Doing to Pete?" *The Magazine of Business* 56 (1928): 140.

38. Williams, *Mainsprings of Men*, p. 44.

39. Williams, *Mainsprings of Men*, p. 266.

40. Williams, *Mainsprings of Men*, p. 244.

41. Williams, *Mainsprings of Men*, p. 185.

42. Williams Tapes, Harry W. Bass Business History Collection, University of Oklahoma, Norman, Oklahoma, cassette number 3, July 24, 1961.

43. Williams, *Mainsprings of Men*, p. 247.

44. Daniel Willard, president of the Baltimore and Ohio Railroad, quoted in Williams, *Mainsprings of Men*, pp. 278–79.

45. Williams, *Mainsprings of Men*, problem 12, p. 77; problem 15, p. 134.

46. Whiting Williams, "Business Statesmanship: A New Force in Business," *The Magazine of Business* 55 (1929): 388–90, 460; Whiting Williams, "What Makes Business an Institution?" *The Magazine of Business* 55 (1929): 658–59, 696–702.

47. Sumner Slichter, "Current Labor Policies of American Industries," *The Quarterly Journal of Economics* 43 (1929): 393–435; *see also* W. K. Donald and E. K. Donald, "Trends in Personnel Administration," *Harvard Business Review* 7 (1929): 143–55.

48. Whiting Williams, "Industrial Relations: A 1930 Survey of the Problem," *Bulletin of the Taylor Society* 15 (1930): 182–88; Williams knew of the studies that had been done by Pennock and others at the Hawthorne plant after Williams left. He agreed with the conclusion of these studies that the type of supervision was more important than the level of illumination and other physical factors.

CHAPTER SEVEN

1. John N. Ingham, *Biographical Dictionary of American Business Leaders*, (Westport, Conn.: Greenwood Press, 1983), vol. 4, pp. 1632–34.

2. Whiting Williams, "Industrial Relations and Hard Times," *Current History and Forum* 34 (1931): 723.

3. Will Rogers, radio broadcast, October 29, 1931, cited in Richard M. Ketchum, *Will Rogers: His Life and Times* (New York: McGraw-Hill, 1973), p. 229.

4. Whiting Williams, "But You Can't Let People Starve," *Survey* 67 (1932): 459–62, 501–3. This "social scar" lasted longer than one generation; *see* Caroline Bird, *The Invisible Scar* (New York: David McKay, 1966).

5. Studs Terkel, *Hard Times: An Oral History of the Great Depression* (New York: Pantheon Books, 1970), p. 5.

6. Whiting Williams, "A Challenge to Industry," *The Annals of the American Academy of Political and Social Science* 154 (1931): 3.

7. Williams, "Industrial Relations and Hard Times," p. 725; *see also* Whiting Williams, "The Worker's Mind Today," *Personnel Journal* 9 (1931): 401–6.

8. Script of radio broadcast, December 10, 1932, Williams Papers, Western Reserve Historical Society, Cleveland, Ohio, container 1, folder 3.

9. Walter S. Gifford, "Cities, Counties, and States Can Handle the Situation," *Survey* 67 (1932): 466 (*see* p. 465 for Allen Burns's position).

10. Whiting Williams, newsletter to selected friends and clients, October 1932, Williams Papers, container 4, folder 1.

11. Whiting Williams, "The Hopeful American Worker," *Saturday Evening Post*, June 17, 1933, pp. 8–9, 87–89. As a cultural note, Williams said that "many communities" had passed ordinances prohibiting anyone from receiving a relief payment until that person surrendered his or her motor vehicle license.

12. Whiting Williams, "The National Recovery Administration and the Worker," *Annals of the American Academy of Political Science* 172 (1934): 64–69. *See also* Whiting Williams, "Our Itinerant Reporter Heard—," *Nation's Business* 22 (1934): 40–42, 98; Whiting Williams, "Getting Labor's Point of View," *The Rotarian* 45 (1934): 9–11. In terms of his assessment of the likelihood of the success of governmental pump-priming, Williams would precede some well-known economists. The unemployment data (Table 7.1) support the view of one school of economic thought, which maintains that President Roosevelt's economic policies did little or nothing to speed economic recovery. In seven years of the New Deal, unemployment never dropped as low as it had been in 1930 and 1931. The most notable decrease in unemployment came only after World War II began: 4.7 percent of the labor force in 1942; 1.9 percent in 1943; and 1.2 percent in 1944. *See* Milton Friedman and Anna L. Schwartz, *The Great Contraction, 1920–1933* (Princeton, N.J.: Princeton University Press, 1965); Robert Heilbroner, *The Making of Economic Society* (Englewood Cliffs, N.J.: Prentice-Hall, 1962), p. 167.

13. Whiting Williams, "The Church in Relation to the Worker," *Annals of the American Academy of Political and Social Science* 165 (1933): 57–63. A contrary point of view in the same issue (pp. 48-56) is by the Christian socialist, Father John A. Ryan, "The Catholic Church and Social Questions." Ryan presents the papal encyclicals of Pope Leo XIII, "On the Condition of Labor" (1891), and Pope Pius XI, "Reconstructing the Social Order" (1931), which articulate the church's position on "reformed capitalism." Father John Ryan was just one of many who carried the idea of social Christianity into the domain of Christian socialism. For a discussion of how the idea of religious reform advocated by Social Gospelist Washington Gladden was tranformed by some into collectivist thinking, *see* James Gilbert, *Designing the Industrial State: The Intellectual Pursuit of Collectivism in America, 1880–1940* (Chicago: Quadrangle Books, 1972).

14. In an unpublished paper, Williams insisted that hard work never made anyone tired, but that not working did. He was referring to the emotional and spiritual aspects of work rather than to its physical aspect. *See* "Labor vs. Leisure or Why Work Anyway?" undated manuscript, probably written in 1933, Williams Papers, container 6, folder 3. A similar thesis is found in Whiting Williams, "Yea, the Work of Our Hands!" *The Rotarian* 47 (1936): 30–33.

15. Whiting Williams, "Russia and Italy Pin Their Hopes on America's Ways of Work," *Nation's Business* 16 (1928): 26–27, 92; Whiting Williams, "What if the Society's Machine Gods Fall Down?" *American Machinist* 74 (1930): 321–24.

16. Williams to Herbert Hoover, July 5, 1933, Williams Papers, container 1, folder 3.

17. Diary entry of August 10, 1933, Kharkov, USSR, Williams Papers, container 5, folder 7.

18. *See* William H. Chamberlin, "The Ordeal of the Russian Peasantry," *Foreign Affairs* 12 (1934): 495–507.

19. Whiting Williams, "The Workers' View of Europe," *Nation's Business* 21 (1933): 19.

20. Diary entry of July 29, 1933, Berlin, Germany, container 5, folder 7. Both of these notions were quite widely accepted at the time. Shirer says, however, that Goering was "cured" of his addiction and that Balder von Shirach, head of the Hitler youth, was a "handsome . . . banal . . . and half-baked" person who wrote poetry in praise of Hitler. The label may or may not have been deserved. *See* William L. Shirer, *The Rise and Fall of the Third Reich* (New York: Simon and Schuster, 1960), pp. 146, 252–53.

21. Williams, "The Workers' View of Europe," p. 53.

22. U.S. Bureau of the Census, *Historical Statistics,* pt. 1, p. 178.

23. James A. Gross, *The Making of the National Labor Relations Board* (Albany: State University of New York Press, 1974). For the "sick chicken" case (*U.S. vs. Schechter Poultry*) that doomed the NIRA, *see* Bernard Bellush, *The Failure of the NRA* (New York: W. W. Norton, 1975), pp. 168–70.

24. Richard T. Ely, *The Labor Movement in America* (New York: T. Y. Crowell, 1886), p. ix.

25. Whiting Williams, " 'Wanted' A Moses — Apply, Fairmount, W. VA.," *Coal Age* 35 (1930): 327–73.

26. Whiting Williams, "The Battle of the Check-Off," *Nation's Business* 25 (1937): 94. At this time, neither Williams nor anyone else really knew how ambitious Lewis was. Lewis was very effective in shielding his private aspirations from his public utterances. He espoused the "working class" notion, but his entire life was spent trying to escape his own miner's origins. He never socialized with his fellow union leaders, preferring businessmen and the socially prominent; he sent his children to Bryn Mawr and Princeton; and at the same time as he was calling on labor to strike for a closed shop, he was seeking admission to the prestigious Cosmos Club of Washington, D.C.! *See* Melvyn Dubofsky and Warren Van Tine, *John L. Lewis: A Biography* (New York: Quadrangle Books, 1977), pp. 285–97.

27. Whiting Williams, "To Join or Not to Join?" *Review of Reviews* 94 (1936): 91.

28. Whiting Williams, "The Sit-Down — A Boomerang?" *American Machinist* 81 (1937): 160–61. Professor Sidney Fine, an established scholar in labor history, presents evidence that the sit-downs at the two General Motors plants in Flint, Michigan, were Communist-inspired and led. The leader at the Fisher body plant was a man who had joined the Communist-controlled Auto Worker's Union in the late 1920s. Lee Pressman, one of John L. Lewis's close advisers, also admitted to having Communist connections. *See* Sidney Fine, "The General Motors Sit-Down Strike: A Re-examination," *American Historical Review* 70 (1965): 691–713.

29. Williams, "The Battle of the Check-Off," p. 92; although the check-off of dues remains legal, the closed shop was outlawed by the Labor Management Relations Act of 1947 (the Taft-Hartley Act). Williams classified the AFL craft unions as "horizontal" unions because the workers were organized by similarities in their crafts; the CIO-type union was "vertical" because it recruited from all skill levels. See Whiting Williams, "Mr. Organizer

vs. Mr. Employer," *Nation's Business* 25 (1937): 33, 83–88.

30. Whiting Williams, "What Do You Mean – 'Check-Off'?" *Nation's Business* 25 (1937): 112.

31. Maurice Isserman, "God Bless Our American Institutions: The Labor History of John R. Commons," *Labor History* 17 (1976): 309–28.

32. Whiting Williams, newsletter to selected friends and clients, April 7, 1939, container 4, folder 2.

33. Whiting Williams, "What the Workers Want," *Scribner's* 103 (1938): 43.

34. Williams, "What the Workers Want," p. 44. Even more recently, Peters and Waterman have identified this practice as an attribute of successful companies – they call it MBWA, or Management by Walking (or Wandering) Around. *See* Thomas J. Peters and Robert H. Waterman, Jr., *In Search of Excellence: Lessons from America's Best-Run Companies* (New York: Harper and Row, 1982), pp. 121–25.

35. Dorothy Rogers Williams, personal conversation, August 19, 1982, Cleveland Heights, Ohio.

36. Herbert Hoover to Williams, August 11, 1934, container 1, folder 3.

CHAPTER EIGHT

1. Cora Burgess (Nashville, Tennessee) to Whiting Williams, September 13, 1934. This and other correspondence about the imposter is in the Williams Papers, Western Reserve Historical Society, Cleveland, Ohio, container 1, folders 3 and 4.

2. Williams to Robert Jorgensen, August 31, 1953, container 2, folder 3. (The Jorgensen correspondence begins in container 2, folder 2.)

3. Harter and Virginia Williams had two daughters, Carol and Martha. Carol married Cyrus W. Brown III and they live in New York City with their daughter, Laura. Carol is a free-lance computer consultant and has published a text in this field. Martha married Dr. Alberto Diaz and they live in Madrid, Spain, with their son, Marcos, and daughter, Caroline. Martha is an interpreter for Random House Publishing in Madrid. Information about the family was provided by Dorothy Rogers Williams in a letter to the author, October 10, 1981, and in an interview on August 19, 1982.

4. Harter Whiting Williams to the author, February 1, 1982.

5. Herbert Hoover to Williams, February 7, 1948, container 2, folder 1.

6. Herbert Hoover to Williams, March 24, 1964; and Williams to Herbert Hoover, August 4, 1964, container 3, folder 1.

7. Whiting Williams, "How Federated Giving – and Planning – Came About" (speech), Williams Papers, container 9, folder 1; correspondence about the event is in container 3, folder 1.

8. Morris S. Viteles to Williams, May 12, 1953, container 2, folder 3.

9. Thomas G. Spates to Williams, January 20, 1960, container 3, folder 1.

10. Thomas R. Brooks, *Clint: A Biography of a Labor Intellectual* (New York: Atheneum, 1978).

11. Clinton S. Golden to Williams, October 31, 1951, and November 26, 1956, container 2, folders 2 and 3.

12. Meredith B. Colket, personal conversation, August 19, 1982, Cleveland, Ohio.

13. A memorial to Hocking is Leroy S. Rouner, ed., *Philosophy, Religion, and the Coming World Civiliation: Essays in Honor of William Ernest Hocking* (The Hague: Marinus Nijhoff, 1966).

14. William E. Hocking to Williams, November 25, 1959, container 2, folder 4. Hocking and Josiah Royce are considered the founders of the American "school of idealistic philosophy." *See* Daniel S. Robinson, *Royce and Hocking: American Idealists* (Boston: Christopher Publishing House, 1968).

15. William E. Hocking to Williams, June 1, 1958, container 2, folder 4.

16. Williams to William E. Hocking, May 8, 1963, container 3, folder 1.

17. Williams to Reinhold Niebuhr, November 7, 1951, container 2, folder 2.

18. M. H. Avery to Williams, November 7, 1951, container 2, folder 2.

19. Williams to M. H. Avery, May 5, 1969, container 3, folder 3.

20. William R. Spriegel and Clark E. Myers, eds., *The Writings of the Gilbreths* (Homewood, Ill: Richard D. Irwin, 1953), pp. 3–65; *see also* Wren, *The Evolution of Management Thought*, pp. 169–80.

21. Allan H. Mogensen, *Common Sense Applied to Motion and Time Study* (New York: McGraw-Hill, 1932); Allan H. Mogensen, *Work Simplification in the Office* (New York: American Management Association, 1938); Allan H. Mogensen, *Work Simplification—The Consultative Approach to Methods Improvement* (Berkeley, Calif: Personnel Management Association, 1951). While some people believe the notion that we should "work smarter, not harder" is a new idea, it in fact came out of Mogensen's Lake Placid Conferences on work simplification over thirty years ago. "Work simplication" was a phrase coined by Erwin H. Schell, a professor at the Massachusetts Institute of Technology, to describe the philosophy and techniques of seeking improvements in work methods. I am indebted to Mr. Mogensen and to Fred J. Kersting of Dallas, Texas, for the information they have provided. Another useful source is Ben S. Graham, Jr., *The Amazing Oversight: Total Participation for Productivity* (New York: AMACOM, 1979).

22. Specific references to the Williams Tapes have been cited earlier. There are eight cassette tapes, recorded at Lake Placid, New York, July 26, 1960; July 24-25, 1961; and at Sea Island, Georgia, January 22-23, 1962. The tapes are now in the Harry W. Bass Business History Collection, University of Oklahoma, Norman.

23. Allan H. Mogensen to author, July 6, 1981.

24. Whiting Williams, "How Is the Welfare State Working Out in England, France and Russia?" (speech delivered before the Economic Club of Detroit, Michigan, February 11, 1957); reprinted in *Vital Speeches of the Day* 23 (1957): 461–66.

25. Williams, "How Is the Welfare State Working Out?" p. 462; Williams Tapes, cassette number 4, July 24, 1961.

26. Williams, "How Is the Welfare State Working Out?" p. 463.

27. Williams, "How Is the Welfare State Working Out?" p. 464, Williams's italics.

28. Whiting Williams, "Human Relations on the Job" (address delivered before the Australian Institute of Management); reprinted in *Industrial Prog-*

29. Williams Tapes, cassette number 2, July 26, 1960.

30. Williams told this story many times. This version, in a Welsh dialect, is in the Williams Tapes, cassette number 5, July 25, 1961.

31. Williams, "Human Relations on the Job," p. 560.

32. Whiting Williams, *America's Mainspring and the Great Society: A Pick and Shovel Outlook* (New York: Frederick Fell, Inc., 1967), pp. 164–71.

33. Jerome S. Auerbach, ed., *American Labor in the Twentieth Century* (New York: Bobbs-Merrill, 1969), p. xx.

34. Eduard C. Lindeman, *Social Discovery: An Approach to the Study of Functional Groups* (New York: Republic Publishing Company, 1924).

35. Jennifer Platt, "The Development of the 'Participant Observation' Method in Sociology: Origin, Myth, and History," *Journal of the History of the Behavioral Sciences* 19 (1983): 379–93.

36. Robert Dubin, "Management: Meanings, Methods, and Moxie," *Academy of Management Review* 7 (1982): 372–79.

37. Ruth S. Cavan and Katherine H. Ranck, *The Family and the Depression* (Chicago: University of Chicago Press, 1938); Mirra Komarovsky, *The Unemployed Man and His Family: The Effect of Unemployment Upon the Status of the Man in Fifty-Nine Families* (New York: The Dryden Press, 1940).

38. Theodore V. Purcell, *Blue Collar Man: Patterns of Dual Allegiance in Industry* (Cambridge: Harvard University Press, 1960), p. xvii.

39. H[yacinthe] Dubreuil, *Robots or Men? A French Workman's Experience in American Industry* (New York: Harper and Row, 1930), pp. 242–44.

40. Stanley B. Mathewson, *The Restriction of Output among Unorganized Workers* (New York: Viking Press, 1931).

41. Donald Roy, "Quota Restriction and Goldbricking in a Machine Shop," *The American Journal of Sociology* 57 (1952): 427–42; Donald Roy, "Work Satisfaction and Social Reward in Quota Achievement: An Analysis of Piecework Incentive," *American Sociological Review* 18 (1953): 507–14; Donald Roy, "Efficiency and 'the Fix': Informal Intergroup Relations in a Piece Work Machine Shop," *American Sociological Review* 60 (1954): 255–66.

42. Sar A. Levitan, ed., *Blue Collar Workers: A Symposium on Middle America* (New York: McGraw-Hill, 1971), p. 3.

43. Studs Terkel, *Working* (New York: Random House, 1972), p. xxiv.

44. John R. Coleman, *Blue-Collar Journal: A College President's Sabbatical* (New York: J. B. Lippincott, 1974), p. 96.

45. E. E. LeMasters, *Blue-Collar Aristocrats: Life-Styles at a Working-Class Tavern* (Madison: University of Wisconsin Press, 1975), p. 19.

46. Robert Saltonstall, *Human Relations in Administration* (New York: McGraw-Hill, 1959), p. 57, italics added.

47. Daniel A. Wren, "Industrial Sociology: A Revised View of Its Antecedents," *Journal of the History of the Behavioral Sciences* 21 (1985): 310–20.

48. Sar A. Levitan and William B. Johnston, *Work is Here to Stay, Alas* (Salt Lake City: Olympus Publishing Company, 1973), p. 7.

49. Alphonse Karr, *in Familiar Quotations of John Bartlett,* 15th ed. (Boston: Little, Brown and Company, 1980), p. 514.

Bibliographic Essay

THE PRIMARY SOURCE of information about Whiting Williams is his papers, which are in the library of the Western Reserve Historical Society, Cleveland, Ohio. These papers were donated in 1969 and were processed by Mark R. Shanahan, who also prepared the register describing the contents. The pages cover the period 1899–1969 and have been organized and preserved in an excellent manner. There are thirteen containers and the entire collection comprises 5.4 linear feet of shelf space. Photographs were removed from the collection and filed in the society's archives as "Family Group 89: Whiting Williams."

Williams's correspondence is in chronological order arranged in the first five containers and covers his business and his personal letters. Included is correspondence with personal friends such as Herbert Hoover, Lowell Thomas, Katherine Wright (sister of the Wright brothers), Reinhold Niebuhr, and Earnest Hocking. His business correspondence covers his speaking engagements, arrangements for travel abroad, and his reports to various consulting clients. Family correspondence fills one container with letters to his family members, some family genealogy, notes on the tragic death of his daughter Carol, and the memorial gifts he made to various libraries, hospitals, and the Carol Williams Scholarship Fund at the Cleveland Institute of Music. This container also has the diaries he kept beginning in 1900 when he was a student in Europe. The diaries were kept rather religiously until 1922 and formed the raw material that appeared in his books and articles. After 1922, there is a gap until the period 1927–1935, and after that the diary record is rather sporadic.

The next five containers contain copies of published and unpublished articles, the manuscripts for these articles, and his lectures and radio talks that were very useful since they exist in no other location. His notes for an autobiography, which was never completed, provide further insights, especially into his early life. The final three containers are a potpourri of materials such as outlines for proposed articles, his work with the Cleveland Federation for Charity and Philanthropy, his interest in parapsychology, his gifts to the Foundation for Research on the Nature of Man, and miscellaneous clippings.

Another exceedingly valuable source of information about Whiting Williams was interviews and correspondence with family members, acquaintances, and colleagues. His widow, Dorothy Rogers Williams, who is now deceased, spent an afternoon with me and answered all of the questions I had about Whiting, his life, their life, and the family. She was a most gracious lady, and the tour of their home in Cleveland Heights, where Whiting lived from about 1922 until his death in 1975, was a touching experience as I examined his library and sat in his favorite armchair. Harter Williams, Whiting's son, also reminisced about his father and various incidents in their family life. In addition to family members, I was able to find others who had known and/or worked with Whiting Williams. James Worthy provided a wealth of information about Williams's technique and message as he spoke to a group at Northwestern University; Fred Kersting, A. B. Cummins, and Meredith B. Colket, Jr., all provided anecdotes and unpublished materials; and Allan H. Mogensen provided a series of cassette tapes of Williams's speeches at work simplification conferences.

While his papers, family, and friends provided a wealth of information, Williams left a publication record that is rarely equalled. He published at least 112 articles and wrote five books: *What's on the Worker's Mind?* (New York, 1920), *Full Up and Fed Up* (New York, 1921), *Horny Hands and Hampered Elbows* (New York, 1922), *Mainsprings of Men* (New York, 1925), and *America's Mainspring and the Great Society* (New York, 1967). The first three books were taken from his diaries of his travels and experiences as a worker. *Mainsprings* resembled a text and built upon the earlier books. Williams's last book, *America's Mainspring*, fell far short of his earlier high standards; only the last chapter on the future had the flashes of perceptiveness that made him such an outstanding observer of people at work.

Other sources filled in the background of the times and travels of Whiting Williams. Since one of his inspirations was Henry C. King, President of Oberlin College, I found Donald M. Love's *Henry Churchill King of Oberlin* (New Haven, CT, 1956) to be very informative. As a student at Oberlin, Williams was influenced deeply by the "Social Gospel," a socially conscious Protestant counterpoint to Social Darwinism. For this influence, I relied upon James H. Fairchild, *Oberlin: The Colony and the College* (Oberlin, OH, 1883); Morrell

Heald, *The Social Responsibility of Business: Company and Community, 1900–1960* (Cleveland, OH, 1970); Jacob H. Dorn, *Washington Gladden: Prophet of the Social Gospel* (Columbus, OH, 1966); Richard D. Knudten, *The Systematic Thought of Washington Gladden* (New York, 1968); John R. Commons, *Social Reform and the Church* (New York, 1894); and Charles H. Hopkins, *The Rise of the Social Gospel in American Protestantism* (New Haven, CT, 1940). From these sources one can piece together the reform movement that characterized America's late nineteenth and early twentieth centuries. Social reform, as in the social work of Graham Taylor (another influential person in Williams's life); political reform as it would evolve from Populism to Progressivism; and industrial reform, such as the ideas of John R. Commons, were all part of the formative fabric that led Williams to seek to understand better and to improve the conditions he observed.

Government documents were useful in corroborating and/or complementing Williams's observations about wages, working conditions, hours of work, the cost of living, union membership, industrial strife, and other facets of the workers' world in which he delved. The best single source is the United States Bureau of the Census, *Historical Statistics of the United States: Colonial Times to 1970* (Washington, DC, 1972). For various investigations into industrial conditions and labor-management relations I relied upon the *United States Commission on Industrial Relations: Final Report* (Washington, DC, 1915); and *Reports of Industrial Conferences, October, 1919 and March, 1920: Annual Report of the Secretary of Labor* (Washington, DC, 1920). An excellent book by Valerie Jean Conner, *The National War Labor Board* (Chapel Hill, NC, 1983), covered organized labor and the administration of President Woodrow Wilson. The Wilson years led organized labor to the heights of aspiration about organizing the unorganized, especially in noncraft work places. These post–World War I years were made more turbulent by a fear of Bolshevism, thus complicating the goals of legitimate, responsible labor leaders such as Samuel Gompers. Excellent studies of this period are by David Brody, *Labor in Crisis: The Steel Strike of 1919* (New York, 1965); Robert K. Murray, *Red Scare: A Study of National Hysteria* (Minneapolis, MN, 1955); and Irving Bernstein, *The Lean Years: A History of the American Worker, 1920–1933* (Boston, MA, 1972).

Williams counted among his friends such labor leaders as Samuel Gompers, long-time president of the American Federation of Labor; Clinton Golden, a ranking official of the United Steel Workers and the

Congress of Industrial Organizations; John P. Frey, president of the Iron Molders; and various others. Williams sought the support of labor leaders, such as getting a letter from Samuel Gompers for permission to become a strikebreaker to study that point of view, and various sources were used to study the history of the union movement and its leadership. Selig Perlman's *A Theory of the Labor Movement* (New York, 1928) postulated that unions were formed because of the "job conscious" needs of the worker to gain access to and control conditions of work, something that Williams had observed earlier. Samuel Gompers was a labor figure who dominated this era and excellent references include: Richard T. Ely, *The Labor Movement in America* (New York, 1886); Selig Perlman and Phillip Taft, *History of Labor in the United States, 1896–1932* (New York, 1935); Phillip Taft, *The AF of L in the Time of Gompers* (New York, 1957); and Samuel Gompers, *Seventy Years of Life and Labor*, 2 vols. (New York, 1925).

Daniel Nelson's *Managers and Workers: Origins of the New Factory System in the United States, 1880–1920* (Madison, WI, 1975) provides an excellent prelude to labor-management relations in the pre-Williams era. Margurite Green's *The National Civic Federation and the American Labor Movement, 1900–1925* (Washington, DC, 1956); Lee K. Frankel and Alexander Fleisher's *The Human Factor in Industry* (New York, 1920); and Henry Eilburt's "The Development of Personnel Management in the United States," *Business History Review* (1959):345–64, are also useful for examining developments before Williams took the train to Pittsburgh to investigate industrial conditions.

The 1920s in American labor-management relations were replete with innovative possibilities for resolving labor-management conflicts and giving workers a greater voice in the workplace. One avenue was that of union-management cooperation and was spearheaded by Whiting Williams's friend Daniel Willard, president of the Baltimore and Ohio Railroad. I found no outstanding work on Daniel Willard; an occasional reference can be found but these are sketchy. Edward Hungerford's *Daniel Willard Rides the Line* (New York, 1938) is fair, but a more definitive work on Willard should be attempted. The subject of union-management cooperation is handled well in both Otto S. Beyer, Jr., *Experiences with Cooperation between Labor and Management in the Railway Industry* (Cambridge, MA, 1929) and Louis A. Wood, *Union-Management Cooperation on the Railroads* (New Haven, CT, 1931). Another pioneering proposal to bring labor and management together went under various labels such as workers' councils, shop councils, or employee representation plans. The pioneering study of these plans was funded by the Russell Sage Foundation and published by Ben W. Selekman, *Sharing Management with the Worker* (New York, 1924). Organized labor did not approve of employee representation plans but saw them as company dominated and antithetical to the interests of the employee. This evaluation is clearly stated in Milton Derber's *The American Idea of Industrial Democracy, 1865–1965* (Urbana, IL, 1970). A counterpoint to that argument and the offered conclusion that employee representation plans were a positive forward step in the development of improved labor-management relations may be found in Daniel Nelson, "The Company Union Movement, 1900–1937: A Reexamination," *Business History Review* (1982):335–57. Another useful overview to the innovative decade of the 1920s is Robert H. Zieger, *Republicans and Labor, 1919–1929* (New York, 1969).

In *The Evolution of Management Thought* (New York, 1979) I had traced developments in management from ancient civilizations up to the present. This provided a perspective that placed Williams in his historical context and provided the opportunity to evaluate his work in terms of the present. Most modern students of work know little of Whiting Williams; I hope this book brings him and his times into a clearer focus.

Index

DEMCO